Teaching
Synthetic
Phonics

Teaching
Synthetic
Phonics

Rhona Johnston and Joyce Watson

Los Angeles | London | New Delhi
Singapore | Washington DC

Los Angeles | London | New Delhi

Learning Matters
An imprint of SAGE Publications Ltd
1 Oliver's Yard
55 City Road
London EC1Y 1SP

SAGE Publications Inc.
2455 Teller Road
Thousand Oaks, California 91320

SAGE Publications India Pvt Ltd
B 1/I 1 Mohan Cooperative Industrial Area
Mathura Road
New Delhi 110 044

SAGE Asia-Pacific Pte Ltd
3 Church Street
#10-04 Samsung Hub
Singapore 049483

Editor: Amy Thornton
Development Editor: Jennifer Clark
Production Controller: Chris Marke
Marketing Manager: Catherine Slinn
Project management by Deer Park
Productions, Tavistock
Cover design: Topics
Typeset by: PDQ Typesetting Ltd

British Library Cataloguing in Publication
data

A catalogue record for this book is available
from the British Library

ISBN 978 1 84445 121 0

Contents

About the authors

Professor Rhona Johnston

After gaining her BA and PhD, Rhona was a learning support teacher for two years. She then joined the School of Psychology at the University of St Andrews, which she left after 20 years to take up a Readership in the School of Psychology at the University of Birmingham. For the past six years she has been a Professor in the Department of Psychology at the University of Hull. Rhona has researched extensively in the areas of reading disorders and reading development.

Dr Joyce Watson

Joyce was an Early Years teacher for a number of years, and then for over 20 years was a lecturer in the Northern College of Education in Dundee. She is now a Research Fellow in the School of Psychology at the University of St Andrews. Joyce holds an MEd from the University of Dundee, her thesis being in the field of reading comprehension. She also holds an Open University Diploma in Reading Development, and a PhD in Psychology from the University of St Andrews. Joyce's thesis was an investigation of the effects of phonics teaching on children's progress in reading and spelling.

Introduction

In 2005 the House of Commons Education and Skills Committee recommended that a study be carried out in England by the Department for Education and Skills (DfES), comparing the effectiveness of synthetic phonics teaching with other approaches such as analytic phonics. In making this recommendation, the committee had reviewed evidence from our study in Clackmannanshire in Scotland, which showed that synthetic phonics teaching led to better reading and spelling than the analytic phonics approach. We found that children who had been taught by the synthetic phonics method not only read and spelt very much above average for their age, but that these gains increased year after year (Johnston and Watson, 2004, 2005a, 2005b). Following on from the Education and Skills Committee's recommendations, the Rose Review (Rose, 2006) was set up to report on the best way to teach young children to learn to read. It concluded that the systematic synthetic phonics approach was the most effective.

The recommendations of the Rose Review led to the publication of *Letters and Sounds* (DfES, 2007), which follows synthetic phonics principles and differs quite markedly from the previous programmes. In *Letters and Sounds* children learn to sound and blend for reading very early on, and spend an equal amount of time on this activity as on segmenting spoken words for spelling. *Progression in Phonics* (DfEE, 1999) uses an analytic phonics approach, introducing blending for reading late on, often at the end of the first year at school, or even at the start of the second year. The supplementary programme *Playing with Sounds* (DfES, 2004) has an earlier introduction of blending for reading, but this is a minor activity compared with segmenting for spelling.

The purpose of this book is three-fold: firstly, to give teachers and trainee teachers the necessary subject knowledge in order to understand the principles behind synthetic phonics, and secondly, to give practical guidance on how to carry out synthetic phonics lessons. Thirdly, our book also explains how to carry out formative and summative assessment, in order that slow learners receive appropriate support early on so that they can catch up with their classmates.

In Chapter 1, we introduce you to the debate about using whole language versus phonics teaching methods, and to the different types of phonics. The terms 'analytic' and 'synthetic' phonics have been much misunderstood, and we have explained what these terms mean in the context of phonics teaching in the UK. We also outline our main findings on the relative effectiveness of these two types of phonics programmes. In Chapter 2 we discuss phonemes – what they are, how children develop an awareness of them, and the role they play in learning to read. In Chapter 3 we describe the Simple View of Reading Model used to underpin *Letters and Sounds*, which has replaced the Searchlights Model that was adopted for *Progression in Phonics*. We also outline Ehri's (2005) model of reading development, which shows you the stages through which children progress to become skilled readers. Chapter 4 explains the principles behind *Letters and Sounds*, in which children learn to read and spell single words by a synthetic phonics approach, but also read captions and sentences from very early on. We also summarise Phases 1 to 6 of *Letters and Sounds*, of which Phases 2 to 6 involve phonics teaching.

Chapter 5 introduces you to the elements of a synthetic phonics programme, describing, for example, how to teach children to blend for reading and segment for spelling. Chapter 6 shows you how to teach a complete synthetic phonics lesson in Phase 2, while Chapter 7 concentrates on how the same structure can be used to teach a lesson in Phase 5. In these two chapters we also suggest how to organise the letter sequence recommended in *Letters and Sound* into weekly lesson plans. Throughout Chapters 5, 6, and 7, we also give guidance on how you can assess the progress your pupils are making, in order to give support early on to those who are progressing more slowly than their classmates.

Chapter 8 follows the progress of a child with special needs, who started school with severe language problems; he made excellent progress once he started a synthetic phonics programme and had a learning programme tailored to his needs. Given the low level of underachievement with a well-implemented synthetic phonics programme, and its effectiveness in helping slow learners, there is no need to resort to remedial programmes based on a whole language approach, such as Reading Recovery. This programme is not compatible with the principles underlying *Letters and Sounds*; it contains only a small amount of phonics for spelling, no phonics for reading, and children are encouraged to use meaning to decode words. In Chapter 9, you will see that the teachers in Clackmannanshire felt very positive about using the synthetic phonics approach, and that they found it to have very beneficial effects on their children's reading and spelling skills.

In conclusion, we hope that this book will help you understand how to implement a synthetic phonics approach to teaching reading and spelling in your classroom. It may seem complex at first, but you will find that it is very simple to adopt as the same lesson format can be used from Reception (Primary 1 in Scotland) right through to the end of Year 2 (Primary 3 in Scotland).

REFERENCES REFERENCES **REFERENCES** REFERENCES **REFERENCES** REFERENCES

DfEE (1999) *Progression in Phonics*. London: DfEE.
www.standards.dfes.gov.uk/primary/publications/literacy/63309/

DfES (2004) *Playing with Sounds: A Supplement to Progression in Phonics*. London: DfES.
www.standards.dfes.gov.uk/primary/publications/literacy/948809/

DfES (2007) *Letters and Sounds*. London: DfES. **www.standards.dfes.gov.uk/local/clld/las.html**

Ehri, L. C. (2005) Development of sight word reading: phases and findings. In Snowling, M. J. and Hulme, C. (Eds), *The science of reading: A handbook*. Oxford: Blackwell, pp135–54.

House of Commons Education and Skills Committee (2005) *Teaching children to read*. Eighth Report of Session 2004–05. London: The Stationery Office.
image.guardian.co.uk/sys-files/Education/documents/2005/04/06/reading.pdf

Johnston, R. S and Watson, J. (2004) Accelerating the development of reading, spelling and phonemic awareness. *Reading and Writing,* 17 (4): 327–57.

Johnston, R. S, and Watson, J. (2005a) A seven year study of the effects of synthetic phonics teaching on reading and spelling attainment. *Insight 17*. (Edinburgh: Scottish Executive Education Department. SSN 1478-6796). **www.scotland.gov.uk/Publications/2005/02/20682/52383**

Johnston, R. S, and Watson, J. (2005b) *The effects of synthetic phonics teaching on reading and spelling attainment, a seven year longitudinal study*. Published by the Scottish Executive Education Department. Available on **www.scotland.gov.uk/Publications/2005/02/20688/52449**

Rose, J. (2006) *Independent Review of the Early Teaching of Reading*.
www.standards.dfes.goc.uk/rosereview/report.pdf

1
What is phonics and which type is the most effective?

Learning objectives

In this chapter you will learn that:

- **whole language approaches to teaching reading were common in the latter part of the twentieth century;**
- **in the 1990s there was concern in England that reading standards were falling because of this approach;**
- **unlike the whole language approach, phonic approaches draw children's attention to the fact that letter sounds provide a good guide to the pronunciation of written words;**
- **with analytic phonics children initially learn some words by sight, followed by learning letter sounds in the initial, the end and finally the middle position of words, and then learning to sound and blend;**
- **with synthetic phonics, children learn a few letter sounds and then learn to sound and blend right away;**
- **research shows that children learn to read and spell much better with synthetic phonics.**

Those recommended for the award of Qualified Teacher Status (QTS) should meet the following Professional Standards:

Q14: Have a secure knowledge and understanding of their subjects/curriculum areas and related pedagogy to enable them to teach effectively across the age and ability range for which they are trained.

Q15: Know and understand the relevant statutory and non-statutory curricula and frameworks, including those provided through the National Strategies, for their subjects/curriculum areas, and other relevant initiatives applicable to the age and ability range for which they are trained.

Introduction

Phonic approaches to teaching reading capitalise on the fact that our spelling system is alphabetic; that is, the letter sounds in words are a helpful, if sometimes imperfect, guide to pronunciation (see the glossary on pages 98–100 for technical terms).

The earliest writing systems were not alphabetic, and indeed an alphabetic system is not well suited to all spoken languages. Very early writing systems used pictures, but obviously such systems are not good at coping with complex ideas as they are limited to picturable objects. Chinese uses a logographic writing system where one character represents a word, and where a sequence of characters forms a sentence. Alphabetic writing systems do the same thing, but here the individual sounds (or phonemes) of the spoken word are represented by letters, and a group of letters forms a word. Early sound-based writing systems, however, used representations at the syllable level, and in Phoenician script syllables were represented by their first consonants. The Greek alphabet was a major development as it introduced letters for each consonant and vowel, which stood for the phonemes in the spoken language. This is what we have in English. Once you have mastered an alphabet like ours, you can read unfamiliar words without having seen them before.

Phonics versus whole language approaches

There has long been a debate about whether children need to be taught that the English spelling system is alphabetic. Early approaches to teaching reading traditionally involved learning letter names or letter sounds (the latter being a major element of the phonics approach). However, a view developed that the phonics approach undermines children's ability to understand what they are reading (Adams, 1990, Chapter 2). The whole language approach to reading developed because of these concerns and also because of a change towards a child-centred educational philosophy. This development was very much influenced by the work of Piaget, who proposed that children were active learners, who constructed knowledge for themselves. These ideas were then applied to reading, although Piaget did not specifically address learning to read in his research, which was largely about the development of logical thinking. According to the whole language view that developed, reading should be meaning based. An unfamiliar word was to be identified as a whole unit by inferring its meaning from the context, or even through picture cues, rather than the 'bottom up' approach of applying phonic knowledge to letters and letter sequences to decode words.

REFLECTIVE TASK

Here are a few short sentences. See if you can work out what the missing words are from the context.

The mouse ran into the _____, and hid under a_____. The cat_____ around and _____ put_____ paws under the _____. _____popped the mouse and it ran into the

_____.

(See the end of this chapter for the answers.)

Whole language methods were in vogue in England for much of the latter part of the twentieth century. The approach moved from being a method where children used their language skills to predict what a word would be from the sentence context, which might aid reading fluency, to an approach whereby this was a major element in developing their word recognition skills. Where the guessed word is incorrect, however, children will get misleading information that will undermine their ability to learn to recognise printed words. This approach is particularly problematical for children with poor language skills, who will have greater difficulty in predicting the missing words, and whose reading problems will therefore be compounded. See Chapter 3 for more about the distinction between reading comprehension and recognising printed words.

What were the perceived problems with phonics? One difficulty was that it involved direct instruction, rather than letting children work things out for themselves. In addition, the type of phonics used in the UK, which was largely of the analytic type (see below), was early on implemented by drilling children in reading lists of similarly spelt words, i.e. word families. These programmes also tended to use phonic readers, some of which used very stilted language. It was argued that the phonic method was unlikely to enthuse children about reading. Another objection to the method was that as some words in the English language are irregularly spelt, the phonic approach cannot be effective and so leads to inaccurate pronunciation. The word 'yacht' is an extreme example of a word that is difficult to read using a phonic approach. However, by the 1980s it was found that the standard of children's reading in England was dropping alarmingly (Turner, 1990), and the lack of phonics tuition was widely considered to be an element in the poor attainment figures. It seemed very likely that some children were not able to work out the alphabetic nature of the English spelling system without explicit tuition, and so made poor progress in learning to read.

Most Scottish primary schools retained phonics teaching, however, although the pace was slowed down as the meaning-based aspect of the reading curriculum took up more and more time. About this time it seemed to us that there was a general lack of knowledge about how phonics was taught, and we decided to examine how it was done in Scottish schools. We began a study in 1992 where we observed the phonics programme from the first to the third year of school in 12 classes (Watson, 1998). The approach used was of the analytic phonics type.

What is analytic phonics?

In analytic phonics, which until recently was the predominant phonic method in the UK, letter sounds are taught after reading has already begun, the children initially learning to read some words by sight. We found in Scottish schools (Watson, 1998) that there was generally a long period devoted to learning the sounds of the letters of the alphabet. This generally started soon after school entry and took until Easter of the first year at school. In this phase, children would typically be shown whole words sharing a common initial letter sound, e.g. 'milk', 'man', 'mother' (Harris and Smith, 1976), with their attention being drawn to the /m/ sound heard at the beginning of the words. The children therefore would have some idea of the usefulness of letters sounds, but only at the beginning of words. They would probably recognise the rest of the word on an holistic basis, as the words presented were often suggested by the children and could be of quite complex structure. For example, a teacher would say 'This is the letter /m/', giving the sound and writing the letter on the blackboard. She would then ask the children for words beginning with the sound /m/, and write these on the board. In one lesson, we observed a little boy say the word 'mallard' (there was a stream nearby), and up it went on the board. After a minute or two there was a whole list of words starting with the letter 'm', listed one under each other on the blackboard. The point of the exercise was to show a family of words all starting with the letter 'm', and there was no attempt to pick words that were easy to read phonically.

We found that when all of the letter sounds had been taught in this way, attention would then be drawn to letter sounds at the ends of words. Finally, children learnt about the vowels in the middle of consonant-vowel-consonant (CVC) words. Although it is often thought that in analytic phonics the sounding and blending of letters to read unfamiliar words is not done, our classroom observations showed that this was a common feature of such programmes. Indeed, in the region in which we were doing the study the teachers had an outline of the progression that their phonics teaching should take, and this was the third step. So towards the end of the first year at school the children in the study were taught to sound and blend CVC words, e.g. /c/ /a/ /t/ → cat.

We were very interested in the fact that our tests showed that once children were alerted to the importance of letter sounds in all the positions in words, independent reading skill really took off. However, in doing studies in other regions in Scotland, we did find by this stage that some schools were not teaching children to sound and blend. We were told that this was because researchers were saying at the time that it was impossible to blend the sounds in a way that made them sound like a word. We do tend to give consonant letter-sounds a following vowel sound, however hard we try not to, so the sounds in a word like 'cat' can come out as /cuh/ /ah/ /tuh/. However, children do manage to make the leap from these sounds to the whole word, perhaps partly because, as they start to sound and blend, a set of known words which look and sound like the unfamiliar word is activated in their memories (Johnston, 1998). The effectiveness of the approach may lie in the fact that the blending procedure teaches children to track through the letters in the word systematically from left to right. As each letter is fixated in turn, the sounds are produced, and this leads to the sequence of letters and sounds for the printed word being closely tied together in memory. This close attention to the letters and their sounds in an ordered sequence in words would inhibit children from looking only at distinctive features, such as end letters or letters sticking up or below the line, which would lead to a primitive form of sight word recognition. The importance of forming a more mature form of sight word recognition well underpinned by sound (or phonological) information will be described in more detail in Chapter 3.

We found that after reading CVC words through sounding and blending, children in analytic phonics programmes spent the next two years learning about consonant digraphs, consonant blends and vowel digraphs. (The term 'digraph' refers to the spelling of one sound with two letters.) The children would typically be shown word families of similarly spelt words, that is, words with consonant digraphs, e.g. 'chin', 'chop, 'chill'; initial consonant blends, 'sting', 'stand', 'stop'; final consonant blends, 'mast', 'lost', 'fist'; vowel digraphs, 'coat', 'boat', 'float'; and split vowel digraphs, 'cake', 'bake', 'make'. Consonant blends (described as adjacent consonants in the Primary National Strategy programme *Letters and Sounds*) would be taught in the second year at school, as would some vowel digraphs, but the really difficult split vowel digraphs such as 'cake' would often be taught in the third year.

We were particularly interested in seeing how this phonic work was integrated with the rest of the reading programme, which had as its major aim that the children understood what they read. Graded readers were generally introduced a month or so after starting school. Although phonic readers used to be widely available, by the early 1990s we found schools were very often using non-phonic reading books in their programmes. We saw little integration of the phonic work and reading for meaning in the first year of school, as the children could not easily apply their phonic reading skills to the reading of books until they had learnt how to sound and blend all through a word. At that point, of course, they could start to read unfamiliar words using this technique, but before that they had to recognise a word by sight, using a form of sight word recognition not well underpinned by letter-sound information.

Phonics in the National Curriculum

In order to improve the teaching of literacy in schools in England, the National Literacy Strategy was started in 1998. A Literacy Hour was established in which teachers were encouraged to teach phonics in addition to the whole language approach. *Progression in Phonics* (DfEE, 1999) was designed for use with children in Reception and Years 1 and 2, and it explained in detail how to implement a systematic phonics programme. As a first step, it was recommended that children be taught listening skills, e.g. to discriminate general environmental sounds, such as vehicle noises, birds singing, water being poured, etc. This progressed to the teaching of phonological awareness, that is, training children to hear rhymes and phonemes in spoken words. The actual phonics programme closely resembled what we had seen being done in Scotland; children being taught letter sounds at the beginning of a word, then at the end, and then ultimately all through the word. At this point, as in Scotland, children were taught to sound and blend letters in order to read unfamiliar words. However, in our studies we found only the faster learning children in England were sounding and blending before the end of the first year at school; most of the children started this procedure at the beginning of their second year at school, which was much later than we had observed in Scotland. The only difference between the actual content of the programmes by this stage was that the children in England were also taught to segment spoken words for spelling. However, we observed no gains for reading and spelling with this additional component, which was often taught in a play-like manner, and seemed to be designed largely to facilitate the development of the awareness of phonemes in spoken words (see Chapter 2 and Chapter 4). After the children had learnt the sounds of the letters of the alphabet, and how to blend and segment CVC words, they then learnt to read and spell words with consonant digraphs, e.g. 'thin'; initial consonant blends, e.g. 'swim'; final consonant blends, e.g. 'tent'. Finally, vowel digraphs were taught, showing, for example, that the vowel sound in 'fine' could also be spelt as in 'high', 'tie', and 'cry'.

A supplementary programme, *Playing with Sounds* (DfES, 2004), was a significant move towards a synthetic phonics approach. It introduced sounding and blending much earlier on, as early as after eight letter sounds had been taught. However, this activity was secondary to segmenting spoken words for spelling via the use of Phoneme Frames. As the children segmented the spoken word phoneme by phoneme in this activity, the appropriate letter would be put in the Phoneme Frame for each sound, working from left to right. Once all the letters were in place, the children then sounded and blended them. This task was also used as the primary means for teaching children letters and their sounds. However, the Phoneme Frame task is not a synthetic phonics technique (see below), it is primarily about segmenting for spelling. Sounding and blending after a word has been spelt is a useful spelling-check process to ensure that the letters in the word are in the right order, but in this context it is not enabling children to read an unfamiliar word as they already know what it is. A clear example of synthesis for reading is the Sound Buttons activity, where the children find out what the word is through blending the letter sounds. However, this task was recommended for introduction into the teaching programme after the Phoneme Frames task, and throughout the programme there were many more references to doing the Phoneme Frame and related tasks, and far fewer to doing the Sound Buttons activity. To add to the confusion between the two tasks, it was suggested that the Sound Buttons task could be used to read the words built up on the Phoneme Frame. Such usage with a known word would mean that this was no longer a synthetic phonics activity.

Huxford (2006) argues that phonics teaching should start with segmenting for spelling as young children are better at this than blending, so starting with segmenting fits the developmental progression. However, although blending is a difficult task, we have found that teaching it early on in the context of printed words is very effective. When it has a secondary role in a programme, children's chances of acquiring the technique will be considerably reduced. Some children are slow to learn how to blend, but they have a better opportunity of understanding the procedure if it is repeatedly carried out in the classroom. While doing this they are also receiving a great deal of exposure to the printed word, and to the importance of using letter sound cues to read unfamiliar words.

There are some other problems with classifying *Playing with Sounds* as a systematic synthetic phonics programme. It should have strongly advised teachers not to tell children to guess unfamiliar words from context or picture cues; this is a whole language approach that undermines the phonic method. The name of the programme gives a clue to another problem – it is primarily play orientated, as was *Progression in Phonics*. In our classroom observations of the latter, the play approach meant that many of the children did not seem to focus on the learning goals of the activity. It would be of interest to know just how effective *Playing with Sounds* was in developing reading and spelling skills, but the DfES did not carry out any testing of the programme's efficacy before launching it. This could have been done by administering standardised reading and spelling tests before and after the programme was carried out, and by comparing attainment with a control group using, for example, *Progression in Phonics*. We have not been able to study the effectiveness of *Playing with Sounds* as we have not found any schools to be implementing it; it was billed as a supplement to *Progression in Phonics* so it is possible that it was not thought by teachers to differ greatly from the previous programme.

Synthetic phonics

If analytic phonics in the UK typically includes sounding and blending for reading, this raises the question of just what is so different about synthetic phonics. It is, as its name suggests, primarily about synthesising letter sounds in order to pronounce unfamiliar words. The critical difference is that with a synthetic phonics approach, shortly after starting school children learn just a few letter sounds and then start to sound and blend right away. Furthermore, new letter sounds are learnt very rapidly; as each new letter sound is learnt the children sound and blend the new words that can be formed with the taught letters. Analytic phonics has a late onset of sounding and blending, or in some cases does not have it at all. Letter sounds are learnt much more slowly and there is a long period in which children are taught letter sounds only at the beginning of words. We can think of phonics teaching as a continuum, with analytic phonics without blending at one end of the continuum and synthetic phonics at the other. The type of analytic phonics done in the UK sits somewhere in the middle, and might be described as analytic-then-synthetic phonics. This is where we would place the *Progression in Phonics* programme, as it had a late onset of sounding and blending. *Playing with Sounds* would be placed closer to synthetic phonics, but it had early sounding and blending as a minor activity, the context of the major activity being segmenting the spoken word for spelling.

In our longitudinal study of analytic phonics in Scotland, we saw that children got a big boost in their independent reading skill when they started to sound and blend towards the end of the first year at school. We then started reading about synthetic phonics, looking particularly at Feitelson's (1988) description of how this is taught in Austria. It has often been said that such an approach for teaching reading works well in German, where there is a very regular spelling system, but that it cannot work in English as we have irregular words such as 'yacht'. If a child tries to sound this out, there might be a 'ch' sound in it, as in 'cheese'. However, 80–90% of words in English do have regular spellings (Adams, 1990). We decided that rather than concluding that an alphabetic approach such as synthetic phonics cannot be effective because of the existence of irregular words in English (Dombey, 2006), the approach should be tested in actual practice.

We now need to look at synthetic phonics in a little more detail (we will describe how to implement it in Chapter 5, 6 and 7). It is a very accelerated form of phonics that does not begin by establishing an initial sight vocabulary. With this method, children are taught some letter sounds before they are introduced to books. After the first few letter sounds have been taught, children are shown how these sounds can be blended together to find out the pronunciation of unfamiliar words (Feitelson, 1988). For example, when taught the letter sounds /s/ /a/ /t/ and /p/ the children can blend the letters in the words 'at', 'sat', 'tap', 'pat', 'pats', 'taps', 'a tap', and so on, to find out what the word is. The children are not told the pronunciation of the new word by the teacher. Thus children can construct the pronunciation for themselves, so this is a self-teaching approach. Most of the letter-sound correspondences, including some vowel digraphs, can be taught in the space of a few months at the start of the first year at school, and consonant blends, such as 'clap', do not need to be taught at all. This means that from very early on children can read many of the unfamiliar words that they meet in text for themselves, without the assistance of the teacher. Although not traditionally part of synthetic phonics, in our studies we did also teach children how to segment spoken words for spelling. There was an equal split between the two activities, and sounding and blending for reading always came before segmenting for spelling in the lessons. Furthermore, the latter activity was not used as a vehicle for teaching the letter sounds. In our studies, children were also taught irregular words from early on, so they soon learnt that some words have a less straightforward relationship with their letter sounds.

Comparisons of the effectiveness of analytic and synthetic phonics teaching

In our studies we measured reading and spelling using standardised tests, where average performance for age is worked out by measuring the skills of representative samples of children. This means that we know how many items in the test a child needs to get right to be performing at the typical level for their age. For example, we used the British Ability Scales Word Reading Test (Elliott et al., 1977) to assess children's ability to read isolated words. There are 90 words in the test, and by counting up the number of words they get correct you can work out a child's reading age; on this test children can score at a level appropriate for a 5 year old, right up to the level expected for a child aged 14 years and 5 months. We measured spelling using the Schonell spelling test (Schonell and Schonell, 1952), which tests children's ability to spell isolated words. We also measured reading comprehension using the Primary Reading Test (France, 1981) until the end of the third year at school, and from then on adopted the Group Reading Test (Macmillan Unit, 2000).

In our study in Clackmannanshire, we examined the effects of three types of phonics programmes on the reading and spelling of children in their first year of school (Primary 1 in Scotland, equivalent to Reception in England). The programmes lasted for 16 weeks, for 20 minutes a day. One group of children learnt by the synthetic phonics approach, another learnt by the analytic phonics approach, and a third group spent half their time doing analytic phonics and half their time learning to blend and segment phonemes in spoken words. All of the children, regardless of the research condition, started reading books six weeks after the start of the programme.

Those children learning by the two analytic phonics programmes read and spelt about right for their age, but the ones learning by the synthetic phonics method were seven months ahead of what would be expected for their age in word reading and spelling (Johnston and Watson, 2004).

It is often said that children who learn to read by a synthetic phonics approach will have difficulty with reading irregular words. We examined this in our study, and found that at the end of the training period the synthetic-phonics taught children read irregular words, such as 'one' and 'said', better than those taught by the analytic phonics method (Johnston and Watson, 2004). We also found that only the children taught by the synthetic phonics approach could read words by analogy at this stage, being able, for example, to work out the pronunciation of 'sing' from the known word 'ring' (Johnston and Watson, 2004).

Synthetic phonics is a fast-moving approach, with letter sounds being taught very rapidly, and with an early start to sounding and blending, whereas analytic phonics is typically slow-moving. It might be the case that if an analytic phonics programme was speeded up, so that letter sounds were learnt equally fast, the children's reading and spelling would be as good as those taught by synthetic phonics. However, we found that this was not the case. Furthermore even after the analytic-phonics taught children learnt to sound and blend they still did not catch up (Johnston and Watson, 2004).

We cannot look at the long-term effects of analytic phonics teaching in the Clackmannanshire study because after our post-testing the children learnt to read using the synthetic phonics method. However, we do have data from a study where we examined analytic phonics teaching for three years. In Figure 1.1 below we compare the long term effects of analytic phonics teaching with the long-term effects of synthetic phonics teaching. (Note that Primary 1 is the equivalent of Reception in England). The left-hand side of the figure shows the children's performance at the end of the first year at school (after both groups had learnt to sound and blend), and the right-hand side shows their performance at the end of the third year at school. To make the graph easy to read we have subtracted the children's chronological ages from their reading and spelling ages. A positive score (where the top of a bar is above the zero line) means that the children have performed above what would be expected for their age. Where the bar is below zero, the children are performing below what would be expected for their age. You can see that the analytic-phonics taught children were behind the synthetic phonics group in word reading and spelling at the end of

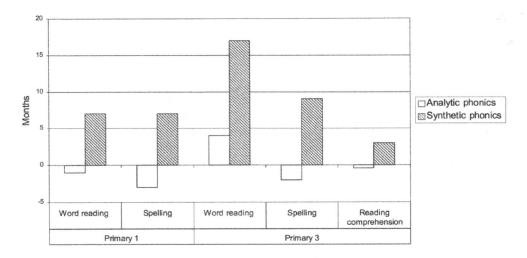

Figure 1.1 Gains in reading and spelling compared with age in Primary 1 and 3, analytic versus synthetic phonics

the first year at school, and were still behind at the end of the third year at school. In many cases, they were also performing below what was expected for their age level. This was despite the fact that the analytic phonics teaching had covered the same ground as the synthetic phonics teaching by the end of the third year at school.

We also found in the Clackmannanshire study that an early start to synthetic phonics led to better results than a later start. When tested at the end of the second year at school, the children who had done synthetic phonics from early on were better at spelling than those who had done analytic phonics first (Johnston and Watson, 2004). A similar pattern was found in word reading for girls, who did better if they had done synthetic phonics early (Johnston and Watson, 2005).

Effects of synthetic phonics teaching on the reading of boys and girls

When we looked at how boys performed compared to girls in our longitudinal study of analytic phonics teaching, we were not surprised to find at the end of the third year at school that they performed less well across the board in word reading, spelling and reading comprehension. Many studies throughout the world have shown that boys read less well than girls (e.g. Mullis et al., 2003). The boys in our longitudinal analytic phonics study read words three months above what was expected for their chronological age, but were four months behind for their age in spelling, and five months behind in reading comprehension. The girls were reading words six months above their chronological age and were age appropriate in spelling and reading comprehension. However, when we saw how the boys performed when learning by the synthetic phonics method at the end of the third year at school we were very surprised. Not only did they do as well as the girls in spelling and reading comprehension (nine months ahead of age in spelling, and three months ahead in comprehension), but they also read words significantly better (see Figure 1.2). Thus, boys read words 20 months ahead of their age, while the girls read around 14 months ahead

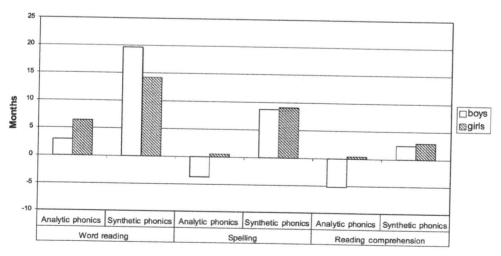

Figure 1.2 Gains in reading and spelling in comparison with age in boys and girls in Primary 3, analytic versus synthetic phonics

(Johnston and Watson, 2005). Both boys and girls read words much better than was the average for their age with synthetic phonics teaching, but the gain was much larger for the boys.

This advantage in word reading for boys was sustained right until the end of our study, being found even when the children were aged 11 and were in the seventh year of school. By that stage, the boys were also significantly better at spelling. Figure 1.3 below shows mean reading, spelling and chronological ages. We do not yet know why this approach is so effective for boys, but there is evidence that they work best in a structured situation (Naglieri and Rojahn, 2001). Synthetic phonics is very structured, and indeed has a 'constructional' element in the way we implement it, even using plastic letters in the early stages (see Chapter 5, 6 and 7), which may particularly suit boys.

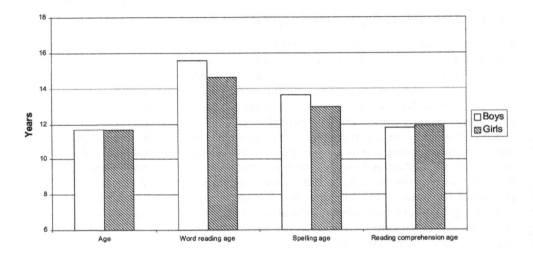

Figure 1.3 Reading and spelling in 11 year old boys and girls taught by the synthetic phonics method

Effects of synthetic phonics on children from areas of deprivation

Research has shown that from the very first year at school, children from areas of deprivation perform less well in reading than those from more advantaged areas (Duncan and Seymour, 2000; Stuart et al., 1998). We found that with synthetic phonics teaching children from less well-off areas only started to fall behind the more advantaged children in word reading, spelling and reading comprehension towards the end of primary schooling (Johnston and Watson, 2005), but even then these comparisons were not statistically significant (see Figure 1.4). By the end of primary schooling, the children from areas of deprivation were reading words six months behind the level of the children from more advantaged areas. However, the children from areas of deprivation were still reading around 38 months ahead of what was expected for their age, and their spelling was 16 months ahead of age level (Johnston and Watson, 2005). Reading comprehension was age appropriate, which is noteworthy as reading comprehension depends on general language skills, and these skills are usually less well developed in children from areas of deprivation.

Over the whole sample, by this stage the children were reading words 42 months ahead of age, spelling was 20 months ahead, and reading comprehension was 3.5 months ahead. In all cases, performance was statistically ahead of what would be expected for chronological age, despite the sample having a verbal ability score of 93 (where the average is 100).

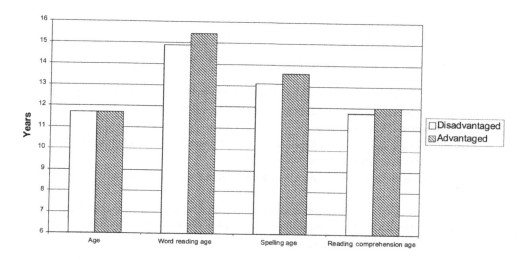

Figure 1.4 Reading and spelling in 11 year old children from advantaged and disadvantaged backgrounds with synthetic phonics teaching

There was also a low level of underachievement. For example, at the end of the second year at school, only 2% of children (regardless of social background) were reading words more than a year below what was expected for their age, and none was as much as two years behind. Even at the end of the seventh year at school, only 13 out of 236 children (5.6%) were reading words more than two years below their age level.

Why is this method of teaching so effective for children from areas of deprivation? Stuart et al. (1998) suggest that one major inequality for such children when starting school is their lack of letter knowledge; these children are less likely to have been carrying out literacy-related learning at home. However, with synthetic phonics this disadvantage is very quickly overcome because of the rapidity with which letter sounds are learnt, producing a level playing field for them.

Another view is that children from areas of deprivation in particular are handicapped by starting school with low levels of phoneme awareness, finding it very hard, for example, to segment a spoken word like 'cat' into phonemes, e.g. /c/ /a/ /t/. Harrison (2004) argues that children will find it impossible to gain much from phonics tuition without prior phonemic awareness ability. In our study in Clackmannanshire, we examined the progress of the children who started school with no phoneme or rhyme awareness skills at all (Johnston and Watson, 2004). After 16 weeks of synthetic phonics teaching, this group scored 45% correct on the phoneme awareness test, whereas the group learning by analytic phonics with an additional phonological awareness training programme scored 22%. Even more importantly, at the end of the second year at school, when all the 'at risk' children had learnt by the synthetic phonics approach, these children were reading words around six months ahead of their chronological age, and were spelling over eight months ahead of their age. You will read more about phoneme awareness in Chapter 2, but we can conclude for the moment that synthetic phonics is very effective at developing phoneme awareness, and does not need to be preceded by a phoneme awareness training programme (carried out without the support of letters and print) in order to get excellent results.

A SUMMARY OF **KEY POINTS**

> English has an alphabetic writing system, and only a small percentage of words are irregular, e.g. 'yacht'.
> Some children do not notice the alphabetic nature of our spelling system without direct tuition.
> A synthetic phonics approach teaches letter sounds very rapidly, an analytic phonics approach teaches them much more slowly.
> A synthetic phonics approach introduces sounding and blending early on, an analytic phonics approach introduces it much later on or not at all.
> Children's reading really takes off when they learn to sound and blend to pronounce unfamiliar words.
> Children learning by the analytic phonics approach did not catch up in reading with those taught by a synthetic phonics approach, even after sounding and blending was introduced.
> Boys read and spell better than girls with synthetic phonics (but girls do very well).
> Children from areas of deprivation keep up with more advantaged children in reading and spelling until near the end of primary schooling, and even then are performing well above what would be expected for their age.
> Synthetic phonics develops phoneme awareness skills better than direct teaching of these skills.

Reflective task answers

The mouse ran into the <u>garden</u>, and hid under a <u>bucket</u>. The cat <u>prowled</u> around and <u>then</u> put <u>her</u> paws under the <u>bucket</u>. <u>Out</u> popped the mouse and ran into the <u>bushes</u>.

REFERENCES REFERENCES **REFERENCES** REFERENCES REFERENCES REFERENCES

Adams, M. J. (1990) *Beginning to Read: Learning and Thinking about Print*. London: MIT.

DfEE (1999) *Progression in Phonics*. London: DfEE.
   www.standards.dfes.gov.uk/primary/publications/literacy/63309/

DfES (2004) *Playing with Sounds: A supplement to Progression Phonics*. London: DfES.
   www.standards.dfes.gov.uk/primary/publications/literacy/948809/

DfES (2007) *Letters and Sounds.* London: DfES.
   http://www.standards.dfes.gov.uk/local/clld/las.html

Dombey, H. (2006) Phonics and English orthography. In Lewis, M., and Ellis, S. (Eds), *Phonics: Practice, Research, Policy*. London: Paul Chapman.

Duncan, L. G. and Seymour, P. H. K. (2000) Socio-economic differences in foundation level literacy. *British Journal of Psychology,* 91, 145–66.

Elliott, C. D., Murray, D. J., and Pearson, L. S. (1977) *The British Ability Scales*. Windsor: NFER Nelson.

Feitelson, D. (1988) *Facts and Fads in Beginning Reading: A Cross-Language Perspective.* Norwood, NJ.; Ablex.

France, N. (1981) *Primary Reading Test*. Windsor: NFER Nelson.

Harris, L. A. and Smith, C. B. (1976) *Reading Instruction: Diagnostic Teaching in the Classroom* (2nd edition). London: Holt, Rinehart and Winston.

Harrison, C. (2004) *Understanding Reading Development.* London: Sage.

Huxford, L. (2006) Phonics in context: spelling links. In Lewis, M., and Ellis, S. (Eds) *Phonics: Practice, Research, Policy.* London: Paul Chapman.

Johnston, R. S. (1998) The case for orthographic knowledge – A reply to Robert Scholes. *Journal of Research in Reading,* 21, 195–200.

Johnston, R. S. and Watson, J. (2004) Accelerating the development of reading, spelling and phonemic awareness. *Reading and Writing,* 17 (4), 327–57.

Johnston, R. S, and Watson, J. (2005) *The Effects of Synthetic Phonics Teaching on Reading and Spelling Attainment, a Seven Year Longitudinal Study.* Publications/2005/02/20688/52449. **www.scotland.gov.uk/**

Macmillan Unit (2000) *The Group Reading Test II.* Windsor: NFER Nelson.

Mullis, I. V. S., Martin, M. O., Gonzalez, E. J., and Kennedy, A. M. (2003) *PIRLS 2001 International Report: IEA's Study of Reading Literacy Achievement in Primary Schools.* Chestnut Hill, MA: Boston College.

Naglieri, J. A and Rojahn, J. (2001) Gender differences in Planning, Attention, Simultaneous, and Successive (PASS) cognitive processes and achievement. *Journal of Educational Psychology,* 93, 430–437.

Schonell, F. J and Schonell, F. E. (1952) *Diagnostic and Attainment Testing* (2nd edition). Edinburgh: Oliver & Boyd.

Stuart, M., Dixon, M., Masterson, J. and Quinlan, P. (1998) Learning to read at home and at school. *British Journal of Educational Psychology,* 68, 3–14.

Turner, M. (1990) *Sponsored Reading Failure: An Object Lesson.* Warlingham, UK: IPSET Education Unit.

Watson, J. (1998) An investigation of the effects of phonics teaching on children's progress in reading and spelling. PhD thesis, University of St Andrews.

2
Phoneme awareness: what is it and what is its role in learning to read?

Learning objectives

In this chapter you will learn that:

- **the phoneme is the smallest unit of sound that changes a word's meaning;**
- **awareness of phonemes is related to letter knowledge and learning to read;**
- **research shows that when phoneme awareness is taught using letters and print it is more effective in developing reading skill than when it is taught on its own.**

Those recommended for the award of Qualified Teacher Status (QTS) should meet the following Professional Standards:

Q14: Have a secure knowledge and understanding of their subjects/curriculum areas and related pedagogy to enable them to teach effectively across the age and ability range for which they are trained.

Q15: Know and understand the relevant statutory and non-statutory curricula and frameworks, including those provided through the National Strategies, for their subjects/curriculum areas, and other relevant initiatives applicable to the age and ability range for which they are trained.

Introduction

What is a phoneme?

The phoneme is the smallest meaningful sound in our language; /c/ and /r/ are different phonemes, so exchanging one for the other turns the word 'cat' into 'rat', which changes the meaning. This is known as *phoneme substitution*; one phoneme is substituted for another, making a new word.

REFLECTIVE TASK

Task 1
How many phonemes do you think there are in spoken English?
(See the end of this chapter for the answers.)

It is important to have a good understanding of phonemes, for both teachers and pupils, as the synthetic phonics method from the very start is based on blending sounds at the phoneme level in order to read unfamiliar words. However, young children do not have much awareness of phonemes in spoken words.

REFLECTIVE TASK

Task 2

Complete the columns below. How many letters are there in each word? How many phonemes?

Words	No. of letters	No. of phonemes
fat	3	3
book	4	3 b/u/k
duck	4	3 d/u/ck
cuff	4	3 c/u/ff
shell	5	3 sh/e/ll
scream	6	5 s/c/r/ea/m
which	5	3 wh/i/ch
phone	6	3 ph/o/ne
yacht	5	3 y/ac/ht
bought	6	3 b/ough/t

See the end of the chapter for the answers. You will have seen that a phoneme can be represented by more than one letter. This is a test of *graphophonemic awareness* skills because you were looking at the printed words. Now try this out on a friend – speak the words (do not let them see this page), and then ask them how many phonemes there are in each word. When you test someone like this without showing them the printed words, you are testing their explicit *phoneme awareness* skills. Do not get upset if you have made some mistakes in doing this exercise, research shows that skilled readers are not perfect at doing this task (Scarborough et al., 1998) and adults can be trained to improve their phoneme awareness skills (Connelly, 2002).

The association between phoneme awareness and reading ability

We know from many research studies that phoneme awareness ability develops closely alongside learning to read words in an alphabetic language (for a review see Adams, 1990). That is, children who read well also tend to have good phoneme awareness skills. To test phoneme awareness in 4 year olds who cannot yet read you would do a test like the reflective task, asking them, for example, what the sounds are in a spoken word such as 'top'. In our work with non-readers (Johnston et al., 1996) we found that some 4 year olds in nursery school were able to recognise initial sounds in words, being able to say 'top' starts with /t/. A few children could even tell us that the sounds are /t/ /o/ /p/. However, this ability to give the phonemes all through the word like this was only found in non-readers who knew many of the letters of the alphabet. In fact, those children who knew no letters of the alphabet were very unlikely to be able to give even one phoneme in a spoken word. This gives us an indication that becoming aware of phonemes is not just a natural skill that children acquire through learning to speak, as it is closely related to learning the alphabet and learning to recognise the printed word.

It has been found, however, that the development of phoneme awareness is not simply a matter of children learning a letter sound and then gaining awareness of that phoneme in spoken words; Hulme et al. (2005) have shown that 5 year olds can show awareness of phonemes for which they do not know the corresponding letter sound or name. However, the children in their study were school age and so must have been learning to read. Once children can read even a few words there are likely to be consequences for their awareness of phonemes; reading may tune children in such a way that they can develop an awareness of phonemes for which the corresponding letter is not known. Even the ability to read the product names on sweet wrappers has been found to be associated with phoneme awareness ability in preschool children. Johnston et al. (1996) found that 4 year olds who could not read in normal print, but who were relatively good at product name recognition (e.g. saying that the writing on a wrapper said 'Smarties'), performed better on a test of phoneme awareness and also had better knowledge of letter sounds/names. Thus these early pre-reading skills showed a complex interaction with each other, and it is difficult to determine causation.

It is important to get the development of phoneme awareness skills into perspective. When looking at Phase 1 of *Letters and Sounds* (DfES, 2007), you might conclude that the development of phoneme awareness ability is a goal in itself and that it needs explicit training without the use of letters. It is of interest therefore that Share et al. (1984) found that tests of phoneme awareness and letter knowledge in young children just starting school were equally predictive of later reading skill, and Share (1995) has further argued that these two skills are of equal importance and are co-requisites for learning to read. As we will see later, there is also evidence that using the synthetic phonics method, where children blend and segment phonemes using letters and words, is particularly effective in developing phoneme awareness.

From large to small units: words, syllables, onset-rimes and phonemes

We need to spend a little time looking at just how spoken words can be split up. They can be segmented into large units such as syllables (e.g. the two syllables in 'walk/ing'), and each syllable can be segmented into the smaller units of onset and rime (e.g. c/at, or st/op, or str/ong). The smallest unit of all is the phoneme level (s/t/r/o/ng).

As you will see from these examples, an onset is made up of the initial consonant or consonants of a syllable:

- the /c/ of cat;
- the /st/ of stop;
- the /str/ of strong.

whereas a rime consists of the vowel and the end part of the syllable:

- the /at/ of cat;
- the /op/ of stop;
- the /ong/ of strong.

REFLECTIVE TASK

Task 3

Complete the columns below, segmenting words into onsets, rimes, and phonemes.

Word	Onset	Rime	Phonemes
dog	d	og	dog
star	st	ar	star
sack	s	ack	sack
crush	cr	ush	crush
snake	sn	ake	snake

See the end of the chapter for the answers. Figure 2.1 below shows a one-syllable word broken down at the onset-rime and then the phoneme level.

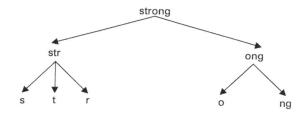

Figure 2.1 Segmenting words into onset-rimes and phonemes

Researchers use the overall term 'phonological awareness' to describe all these different levels of segmenting the spoken word, the smallest unit being the phoneme level (s/t/r/o/ng). To explain the various levels of segmentation we have to show you the words and letters in *print*, as in the figure above, but what we are talking about here is knowledge about the sounds in *spoken* words.

Do children's phonological skills develop from awareness of large units and then move on to progressively smaller units?

There is a view that it is necessary to teach children about larger units such as syllables and rhymes first and then later on to teach them about the smaller phoneme units. This comes from the idea that before they learn to read children find it easier to hear larger units of sounds, such as syllables and rhymes, and that small units such as phonemes are much harder for them to detect in spoken words.

This view is based on research that proposes that children show a developmental progression from first of all being aware of large units in speech, and then becoming aware of increasingly smaller units, showing the progression syllable → onset-rime → phoneme awareness (Treiman, 1987; Metsala and Whalley, 1998). According to this view, what comes most easily to young children before learning to read is hearing syllables in words, as they find it easier to tap to the syllables in words, e.g. two taps for 'cowboy', than to tap to the phonemes in words, say three taps for 'cat' (Liberman et al., 1974). This progression is thought to be the same across all languages, and to be internally driven by an increasing vocabulary (Metsala and Whalley, 1998). The argument is that as children learn more and more spoken words, they need to be able to make finer and finer discriminations in order to detect the differences between similar-sounding words. It is thought that early on children represent words at the whole-word level, and then break them down into smaller elements as their vocabulary knowledge develops. As the catalyst for change is seen as being vocabulary development, it is thought that before starting reading tuition it is a good idea to expand children's spoken vocabularies in order to develop their phoneme awareness skills (Rose Review, 2006). However, this is an indirect and time-consuming method of developing phoneme awareness, so we need to be sure that this would be time well spent. It is of course highly desirable to develop children's vocabulary knowledge, but it should also be borne in mind that the reading of books is also a very effective way of achieving this.

Children develop awareness of small units earlier than previously thought

Gombert (1992) has alternatively argued that it is *language* development rather than *vocabulary* development that affects phonological development, which means that the characteristics of the child's native language will affect the process. Furthermore, according to his view there are also external factors that influence phonological development, of which a major one is learning to read. Duncan et al. (2006, Experiment 2) used a task where children aged from 4 years upwards had to say which sound was the same in pairs of words. This is a more explicit test of phonological awareness than tapping the number of sounds in words. The children identified syllables, initial phonemes or rhymes in lists of pairs of spoken words, after hearing a puppet demonstrate the phonological unit required for each list. Duncan et al. (2006) found that 4 year old French children who were non-readers were indeed better at identifying syllables than phonemes and rimes at this age, but English-speaking children actually identified phonemes a little better than syllables and rimes. Furthermore, the ability to identify an initial shared phoneme increased greatly in the English-speaking children once they started to learn to read using a phonic approach at age 5. The French children's ability to identify phonemes also increased greatly when they started to learn to read at the age of 6 years old using a phonic approach. These findings point to learning to read as being a very important factor in developing phoneme awareness.

In one of our studies (Johnston et al., 1996) we expected, because of the prevailing view that rhyme skills develop before phoneme awareness skills, that preschool children would be good at producing rhymes compared to saying the phonemes in spoken words. However, on average these 4 year olds only scored 24% correct in a task where we asked them, for example, for a word that rhymed with 'hop'. In fact, we noticed that they often produced an alliterative response instead, saying a word beginning with the same sound, e.g. 'hat'. Furthermore, in a task where they had to say what sounds there were in spoken words, the score was 23% correct for the first phoneme in words, e.g. saying that 'top' starts with /t/. Thus their level of performance on this task was very similar to their performance on the rhyme task.

Phonological awareness training and *Letters and Sounds*

Letters and Sounds (see Chapter 4) recommends that you develop children's phonological awareness skills in Phase 1, before starting a synthetic phonics programme in Phase 2. Indeed, not only does *Letters and Sounds* recommend that children orally sound and blend phonemes to produce words (and to segment phonemes in spoken words) before they get started on learning to read via a synthetic phonics programme, it proposes that these activities should be continued throughout Phase 2. It is important to consider therefore how children become aware of phonemes all through the word.

The studies cited above have shown preschool children to have quite surprisingly good awareness of the phonemes as the beginning of words (i.e. onsets), but most of them are not very adept at giving the phonemes in other positions in words. It may seem logical to conclude from this that training children in blending and segmenting phonemes in spoken words without showing letters would be beneficial for developing their phoneme awareness skills all through the word and so speed up learning to read.

However, after carrying out a major review of the literature, Castles and Coltheart (2004) have concluded that no study has established that phoneme awareness training on its own assists reading development, whereas there is overwhelming evidence that when phoneme awareness is taught in the context of letters it has a positive effect on learning to read. They argue that only a few studies are suggestive of a causal link between phoneme awareness training without letters and improved literacy skills, and that these studies are open to question because they were, for example, carried out on children who may have had some knowledge of the alphabet and/or were at school and already learning to read.

Leaving aside Castles and Coltheart's (2004) methodological criticisms of the studies that claim to find phoneme awareness training on its own to be beneficial in developing reading skill, it is possible to assess how useful training phoneme awareness is on its own compared to learning about phonemes at the same time as learning about letters. Ehri et al. (2001), in a meta-analysis of 52 studies for the US National Reading Panel, showed that when phoneme awareness was taught using letters this was statistically more effective in developing reading skill than when it was taught without letters.

It is interesting to look in detail at some UK studies that have examined the effects of phonological awareness training on children's reading skills. Hatcher et al. (1994) found that 7 year old poor readers who received a phonological awareness training programme in a separate session to their reading lesson did indeed improve their performance on a test of phoneme awareness, but their reading skills were no better than a group that did not get this intervention. Similarly, we found in our study in Clackmannanshire (Johnston and Watson, 2004) that normal school entrants learning to read by an analytic phonics programme scored 17% correct (up from 4.5%) on a test of all-through-the-word phoneme awareness at the end of the programme. A second group had an analytic phonics programme that was supplemented by daily lessons on blending and segmenting phonemes without using letters and print, and they scored 35% correct (up from 2.7%); this was better than that of the first group, but this difference was not statistically significant. However, a third group was taught to read by a synthetic phonics method where the children learnt to blend and segment phonemes all through the word in the context of letters and print. Their score on the phoneme awareness task was 4.1% correct before they did the synthetic phonics programme, and 65% correct at the end of the programme. Their performance was significantly better than that of the first and second group. Of particular interest is the fact that the second group had training on phonemes all through the word *without letters*, but were found to have nearly half the level of phoneme awareness of the synthetic phonics group, who had had similar training *with letters*. These data are shown in Figure 2.2.

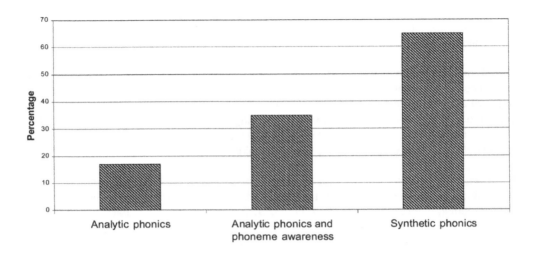

Figure 2.2. Phonemic awareness ability in March of first year at school, Clackmannanshire study

Furthermore, what is really important is how well the children read. At the end of the study, the synthetic phonics group read seven months ahead of the two analytic phonics groups, and spelt eight to nine months ahead. The analytic phonics group that had a supplementary phoneme awareness training programme did not read or spell better than the group that just did analytic phonics, despite having higher levels of phoneme awareness ability. These findings support the conclusion that Ehri et al. (2001) drew from their meta-analysis – it is much better to learn about phonemes in the context of letters and print. Phonemes are a very abstract concept, but when taught with letters and print, children have concrete visual representations of the sounds and these support their learning.

A SUMMARY OF **KEY POINTS**

> Studies have shown that contrary to the idea that children at first become aware of large units such as rhymes, and only later become aware of smaller units such as phonemes, preschool children's phoneme awareness skills are as good as their rhyme skills.

> Children's preschool phoneme awareness ability is associated with early literacy skills, e.g. a knowledge of letters of the alphabet and the ability to recognise environmental print such as the product names on sweet wrappers.

> Children learn phoneme awareness better in the context of letters and print compared to learning without this concrete visual support.

> Children who learn phoneme awareness using letters and print develop significantly better reading and spelling skills than those who do not.

Reflective task answers
Task 1 – Phonemes

The total number of distinct sounds in spoken English vary with accent, but it is generally agreed that there are 40+.

If you answered 26 to this question, you were thinking of the number of letters in the alphabet. We do not have a letter for every sound in English, which is why we have to double up letters, particularly for vowels, e.g. 'coat', 'feet'. Spellings like 'oa' and 'ee' are called vowel digraphs. There are also consonant digraphs, e.g. 'ship', 'chop'. For both vowel and consonant digraphs, we use two letters to stand for one sound.

Task 2 – Segmenting words into phonemes

Words	No. of letters	No. of phonemes	Phoneme splits and their associated spellings
fat	3	3	/f/ /a/ /t/
book	4	3	/b/ /oo/ /k/
duck	4	3	/d/ /u/ /ck/
cuff	4	3	/c/ /u/ ff/
shell	5	3	/sh/ /e/ /ll/
scream	6	5	/s/ /c/ /r/ /ea/ /m/
which	5	3	/wh/ /i/ /ch/
phone	5	3	/ph/ /o/ /ne/
yacht	5	3	/y/ /ach/ /t/
bought	6	3	/b/ /ough/ /t/

Task 3 – Segmenting words into onsets, rimes, and phonemes

Word	Onset	Rime	Phonemes
dog	d-	-og	/d/ /o/ /g/
star	st-	-ar	/s/ /t/ /ar/ or /s/ /t/ /a/ /r/
sack	s-	-ack	/s/ /a/ /ck/
crush	cr-	-ush	/c/ /r/ /u/ /sh/
snake	sn-	-ake	/s/ /n/ /a/ /k/

REFERENCES REFERENCES **REFERENCES** REFERENCES REFERENCES REFERENCES

Adams, M. J. (1990) *Beginning to Read: Learning and Thinking About Print*. London: MIT.

Castles, A. and Coltheart, M. (2004) Is there a causal link from phonological awareness to success in learning to read? *Cognition*, 91: 77–111.

Connelly, V. (2002) Graphophonemic awareness, in adults after instruction in phonic general-isations. *Learning and Instruction* 12 (6): 627–49.

DfES (2007) *Letters and Sounds*. London: DfES. **www.standards.dfes.gov.uk/local/clld/las.html**

Duncan, L. G., Cole, P., Seymour, P. H. K. and Magnan, A. (2006) Differing sequences of metaphonological development in English and French. *Journal of Child Language*, 33: 369–99.

Ehri, L. C., Nunes, S. R., Willows, D. M., Schuster, B. V., Yaghoub-Zadeh, Z. and Shanahan, T. (2001) Phonemic awareness instruction helps children learn to read: Evidence from the National Reading Panel's meta-analysis. *Reading Research Quarterly,* 36: 250–87.

Gombert, J. E. (1992) *Metalinguistic Development.* London: Harvester Wheatsheaf.

Hatcher, P. J., Hulme, C. and Ellis, A. W. (1994) Ameliorating early reading failure by integrating the teaching of reading and phonological skills: the phonological linkage hypothesis. *Child Development*, 65: 41–57.

Hulme, C., Caravolas, M., Malkova, G. and Brigstocke, S. (2005). Phoneme isolation ability is not simply a consequence of letter sound knowledge. *Cognition*, 97: B1–B11.

Johnston, R. S., Anderson, M. and Holligan, C. (1996) Knowledge of the alphabet and explicit awareness of phonemes in pre-readers: the nature of the relationship. *Reading and Writing*, 8: 217–34.

Johnston, R. S. and Watson, J. (2004) Accelerating the development of reading, spelling and phonemic awareness. *Reading and Writing*,17 (4): 327–57.

Liberman, I. Y., Shankweiler, D., Fischer, F. W. and Carter, B. (1974) Explicit syllable and phoneme segmentation in the young child. *Journal of Experimental Child Psychology*, 18: 201–12.

Metsala, J. L. and Walley, A. C. (1998) Spoken vocabulary growth and segmental restructuring of lexical representations: precursors to phonemic awareness and early reading ability. In J. L. Metsala and L. C. Ehri (Eds) *Word Recognition in Beginning Literacy*. Mahwah, NJ: Erlbaum.

Rose, J. (2006) *Independent Review of the Teaching of Early Reading: Final Report.* Nottingham: DfES.

Scarborough, H. S., Ehri, L. C., Olson, R. K., Fowler, A. (1998) The fate of phonemic awareness beyond the elementary school years. *Scientific Studies of Reading*, 2: 115–43.

Share, D. (1995) Phonological coding and self-teaching: *sine qua non* of reading acquisition. *Cognition,* 55, Section 4: 190–96.

Share, D. L., Jorm, A. F., Maclean, R., and Matthews, R. (1984) Sources of individual differences in reading acquisition. *Journal of Educational Psychology*, 76: 1309–24.

Treiman, R. (1987) On the relationship between phonological awareness and literacy. *Cahiers de Psychologie Cognitive*, 7: 524–9.

3
How does reading develop?

Learning objectives

In this chapter you will learn that:

- **the Primary National Strategy has adopted the Simple View of Reading;**
- **according to the Simple View, reading comprehension is composed of two processes, recognising the printed word and understanding spoken language;**
- **word recognition becomes increasingly underpinned by sound information as reading skill increases.**

Those recommended for the award of Qualified Teacher Status (QTS) should meet the following Professional Standards:

Q14: Have a secure knowledge and understanding of their subjects/curriculum areas and related pedagogy to enable them to teach effectively across the age and ability range for which they are trained.

Q15: Know and understand the relevant statutory and non-statutory curricula and frameworks, including those provided through the National Strategies, for their subjects/curriculum areas, and other relevant initiatives applicable to the age and ability range for which they are trained.

Introduction

The Simple View of Reading

It is obvious that we cannot read if we are not able to recognise words on the printed page. If this page was printed in the Greek alphabet many of us would not be able to say what even one word was, let alone get the full meaning. So there are two aspects to reading – recognising the words and getting meaning from the sentences. Although most children starting school cannot recognise the printed word, they understand much of what is said to them. That is, they start school with *linguistic* comprehension. If they learn to read a few words after starting school, such as 'the', 'cat', 'sat' ,'on', 'the', 'mat', understanding the resulting sentence would easily be within their comprehension abilities, and they would be able to draw a picture of this for you after reading it.

Although reading comprehension is a very complex skill, according to Gough and Tunmer (1986) in their Simple View of Reading it can be reduced down to two components:

- **recognising and decoding printed words;**
- **linguistic comprehension – the ability to understand spoken language.**

Studies have shown that separate measures of word recognition (decoding) and linguistic comprehension together give a good account of how well children comprehend what they read (Hoover and Gough, 1990). This means that, by and large, *reading comprehension ability* (R) can be predicted by taking *decoding* (D) and *linguistic comprehension ability* (C) together:

$$R = D \times C.$$

Despite this there has been a view that learning to decode is not important (Goodman, 1973; Smith, 1982), and this view has been very influential in the English-speaking world. Thirty or so years ago it was believed that when a skilled adult reads he or she does not take in all the printed words on the page, and gets meaning largely by getting the gist of what is written. However, since then it has been shown by studying eye movements that we do indeed sample pretty much every word on the page. Guessing from context is what *unskilled* readers do, because of their inability to recognise all the words (Stanovich, 1980). It does not mean that it is a good way to read or that we should teach children to do that. It is actually quite hard to get a missing word by guessing, e.g. 'Jack went for a ....'. This could be a walk, a swim or even a pizza! Children's reading progresses much better if they have a method for working out what an unfamiliar word is, rather than guessing, looking for pictures cues, or asking the teacher. This means that the flow of reading is not broken up, which helps children to get the meaning from what they are reading. In a study where one group of children had systematic instruction in phonics, where they used letter sounds to decode words, and the other group learnt to read by a comprehension approach, where words were guessed from context using the initial letter of the word as a clue, reading comprehension was actually better in the phonics taught group (Connelly et al., 2001).

Children can have problems with either word recognition or listening comprehension, or indeed with both areas. There is much evidence that dyslexic children have a primary problem in recognising the printed word, and indeed one influential definition of dyslexia is that it is *a specific language-based disorder of constitutional origin characterised by difficulties in single word decoding* (Orton Dyslexia Society, 1994). However, there are also children who have adequate word recognition abilities, but have difficulty in comprehending what they read (Cain and Oakhill, 2004).

The Primary National Strategy (2006) represents the simple view of reading in a chart like the one below (see Figure 3.1). A child may have poor word recognition skills, but despite this if a text is read out to them that child may show good understanding of the meaning. However, another child may have good word recognition skills and yet have poor understanding of a text when it is read out loud. Another child may have poor word recognition skills and poor comprehension of a text when it is read out loud. Finally, a child can be good in both areas. These are of course extremes on any of these dimensions, and a child's performance may lie at any point on the continuum, but in showing the extremes the point is that when you are teaching your pupils to read, they will not necessarily progress equally fast in both areas. Separating out these two dimensions draws our attention to the fact that children's progress in these two areas needs to be monitored and assessed, so that if they fall behind they can receive extra help to enable them to catch up.

The purpose of introducing synthetic phonics teaching early on in primary schooling is to eradicate as far as possible the problems children have in recognising the printed word, in order to allow more time in the curriculum for developing a comprehension of what they read.

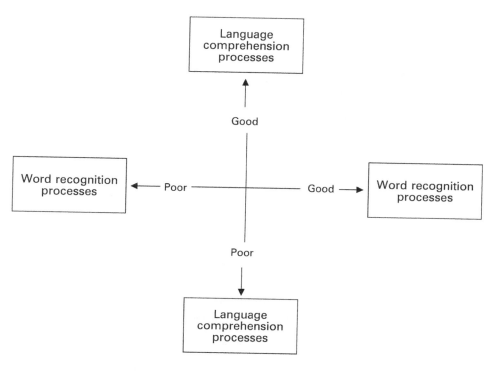

Figure 3.1 The simple view of reading

How do children learn to recognise the printed word?

We know that, as skilled readers, when we move our eyes from left to right across the page we rapidly gain the meaning of each word, and so make sense of the text. But how do we come to be able to recognise the words?

For some children, a few exposures to a printed word and its meaning are enough to secure that word in their memory. It is unlikely that these children are just using the visual pattern the word makes; many words are visually similar because we only have 26 letters in the alphabet. Young children who think that recognising words means looking at the shape will learn some words, but as they learn more words they will soon find it difficult to distinguish them from similar looking ones. To varying extents (the amount depending on the method by which they have been taught), children learning to read in English will use information from the sounds that the letters represent. We know that some children can work out the alphabetic code for themselves. Children learning to read using the official scheme in New Zealand, for example, where only the names of the letters of the alphabet are taught, can read 'made up' or 'nonwords', such as 'poast', that they have never seen before (Johnston and Thompson, 1989). However, they read nonwords less well than phonics taught children, and a substantial number of children in New Zealand join the Reading Recovery programme at the age of 6, as they need extra help with reading.

Before looking at phonics teaching in later chapters, we need to look at what we know about how children's ability to recognise words develops. When children start school their cognitive and perceptual skills are still developing and they are unlikely to be able to recognise words in the way an adult would.

A model of sight-word reading development

One very influential model of reading development (Ehri, 2005) encompasses the thinking of other major theorists, and has been tested extensively over a long period of time. This model looks closely at the development of sight-word reading, and how that changes over time (see Table 3.1).

Table 3.1 Ehri's Model of Reading Development

Phases	Main characteristics of word reading	Examples
Pre-alphabetic phase	Child reads by salient visual cues and does not look at letters	Reads 'Xepsi' as 'Pepsi' if presented within its distinctive logo
Partial alphabetic phase	Child uses some letter sound information	Reads 'tin' as 'toy', reads 'jail' as 'jewel'
Full alphabetic phase	Child makes connections between letters and sounds all through the words, including vowels	Reads an unfamiliar word, e.g. 'dog', by converting letters into sounds all through the word
Consolidated alphabetic phase	Child recognises large elements such as morphemes	Recognises 'dance' and 'ed', so can read 'danced' on the basis of these two units

When teaching children who have got going with reading, it is evident that they know some words by 'sight', that is, they look at them and instantly know what they are. Less familiar words have to be worked at, by blending the sequence of letter sounds, i.e. a synthetic phonics approach, or perhaps by making analogies with other known words, e.g. reasoning that 'date' looks like 'late' but starts with 'd' (using a form of phonics which uses sounds units larger than the letter-sound level). We know quite a lot about phonics or phonological approaches to reading, but relatively little about how 'sight'-word reading is carried out. It has been thought for a long time that sight-word reading in a skilled adult reader is largely visual, e.g. based on letter patterns or perhaps even word shape, with little or no information about letter sounds being activated. Ehri reasoned that if children need to use letter sound information while they are learning to read unfamiliar words, it would be surprising for that just to wither away as they become more skilled. She proposes that even when an adult is seeing a familiar word, information about its visual appearance, meaning and sound is all likely to be generated, although the sound information would not be actually needed to pronounce familiar words. Ehri also proposes that sight-word reading changes as reading skill increases. She suggests that in the very earliest stages of recognising print, children do indeed take a very visual approach, but that as their reading skill progresses their word recognition becomes more and more underpinned by the sounds.

One way to examine developmental change is to describe phases or stages in the development of the skill. Development is complex and dynamic, whereas when we describe stages they sound simple and static. We use stage theories as a way of getting a handle on the complexities of how skills are developing, taking a snapshot of what is going on in a child's reading at one particular point in time. When we do put children's reading under the microscope in this way, we find there are great similarities in what children are doing, even though as teachers what you will see looks more like diversity. The approaches taken by children in a class may look diverse to the teacher, as if they are learning to read in a different way, but they are generally at a slightly different point on the same developmental pathway.

Ehri has studied this developmental pathway by examining phases in reading development, looking at how printed words are being stored in memory at a particular point in time.

Pre-alphabetic phase

Here Ehri found the approach taken to be very visual. Children focus on a salient visual cue in the word, or even something external to the word, like a thumbprint! Ehri found that early on children could 'read' a word like Pepsi (when presented within its distinctive logo), and even if a letter was changed so it read Xepsi, many of the children would identify it as Pepsi. This was despite the children knowing 60% of the names of the letters of the alphabet. The logos surrounding such words do act like the thumbprint, that is, it is an external or contextual cue that draws the child's attention from the actual print.

It has been found, however, that nursery children do have some success in identifying words like 'Smarties' if the word is presented in its distinctive print, but with the logo information removed. However, the children generally cannot recognise such a word when it is presented in normal print (Johnston et al., 1996). So children in this phase generally use visual cues to recognise words even if they know a few letter names or sounds, as they do not know how to use that information. We can conclude that preschool children are very aware of print in their environment, especially when it helps them identify a favourite chocolate bar, but the way they recognise it is a long way from the alphabetical reading they develop once they start to learn to read at school.

Partial alphabetic phase

This phase emerges when children can relate letter sounds to printed words. However, at this stage they cannot work all the way through the letter sounds in words in order from left to right. You can get a feel for how a child is dealing with print through the errors he or she makes. For example, if the child can recognise the word 'toy', when faced with the word 'tin' they may fix on the 't' and think they are seeing the word 'toy'. So this is a partial alphabetic approach.

This type of error is very common when children are learning by an analytic phonics approach, if they are at the stage where letter sounds are taught only at the beginning of words. As their reading skill progresses, children may recognise the beginning and end letters, reading the word 'jail' as 'jewel'. Again, such an approach may be facilitated by analytic phonics teaching, which follows up teaching letter sounds in the initial position of words by drawing children's attention to the role of letter sounds at the ends of words. So in this phase sight-word reading is becoming more closely tied to the sounds of the letter in the words.

Full alphabetic phase

In this phase children are able to make connections between letters and sounds all through the word. To be able to read like this, children now need to convert the vowel letters into sounds. In analytic phonics, towards the end of the first year at school, simple vowels, as in words like 'cat', 'dog', and 'tap', are taught in the middle of words. This means that faced with an unfamiliar CVC (consonant-vowel-consonant) word, the children can work out for themselves how to read it. This is particularly the case if they are taught to sound each letter in sequence from left to right and blend the sounds together. So faced with an unfamiliar word, they can work out the sounds for each letter, e.g. p-a-t, and then blend them to find that the word is 'pat'. This approach is taught right from the start in synthetic phonics.

So far we have been talking about letter-sound correspondences, but written English often represents sounds with more than one letter. Our spelling system is largely phoneme-based. What is a phoneme? A phoneme is the smallest unit of sound that changes a word's meaning. So we can change the spoken word 'cat' into 'rat' just by changing the first phoneme, which in this case means changing a single letter. Other phonemes are not so simple in spelling, and can be made up of several letters. For example, we write the sound 'sh', and the long 'o' sound in 'coat', with two letters. 'Sh' is a consonant digraph and 'oa' is a vowel digraph; these are phonemes in speech and graphemes when written down. However, some words in English are irregularly spelt, and are not amenable to such a straightforward mapping between graphemes and phonemes.

For a long time it was thought that these words were read visually. However, even the word 'yacht' provides some guide to pronunciation through its initial and final letters. We know that children probably do use letter sound connections even with these words, as there is such a high association between children's ability to read regular and irregular words (Stuart and Masterson, 1992). However, the strategy of converting graphemes into phonemes from left to right with words like this will lead to errors, so identification of these words has to rely to a certain extent on word specific knowledge.

This phase is a very enabling one for children to reach, as they now have the means to teach themselves how to pronounce a lot of the new words they meet. But as skilled readers we know that when we have worked out what a word is, we do not need to go through the laborious process of decoding it each time – we will recognise it instantly.

Consolidated alphabetic phase

This brings us to the final phase of Ehri's model. Ehri argues that we develop recognition of larger elements such as morphemes, that is, meaning-based units. For example 'danced' is composed of the root morpheme 'dance' and the grammatical morpheme '-ed'. We also recognise onsets, which can be single phonemes (e.g. 'c' in 'cat', 'sh' as in 'shop'), or several phonemes (and therefore several graphemes), such as 'str' in 'string', and we also recognise rimes, such as 'ing' in 'string'. Once we can read the word 'string', when we meet words like 'king' and 'thing' we can recognise the 'ing' segment as a whole unit. So when we meet an unfamiliar word, we may not need to go to the grapheme level to work out how to pronounce it, we may be able to use larger chunks. There will also be one syllable words that are so familiar that we can recognise them instantly on sight, without making analogies with other words.

However, Ehri does not think that we ever come to a stage where we read words purely visually – that is, however familiar we are with a word, when we recognise it we draw from our memory its meaning, its whole word pronunciation, and all the connections between letters and sounds (e.g. its connections to letters at the phoneme, onset and rime levels). What we do not need to do any longer is laboriously build up the pronunciation of the word from the graphemes by blending or by making an analogy with another word. So this final phase is also sight-word reading, but it is *paved with phonological information* (Ehri, 1992).

REFLECTIVE TASK

Phases of reading development

Observing children showing the following patterns of reading, in which column would you place each child? Enter a number for each child. They may be in more than one phase, pick the most likely one.

1. Child reads 'Ribena' on the bottle but cannot read it in normal print.
2. Child reads 'kicking' without sounding and blending but has not seen this combination of morphemes ('kick' and 'ing') before.
3. Child reads 'Kit-Kat' on a packet and can sound and blend 'kitkat' when it is presented in normal print
4. Child reads 'pill' for the word 'pail' – both words presented in normal print.

Pre-alphabetic	Partial alphabetic	Full alphabetic	Consolidated alphabetic

(See the end of this chapter for the answers.)

Synthetic phonics and phases in reading development

When children learn by the synthetic phonics approach, the partial alphabetic phase is by-passed. Typically in a synthetic phonics programme, children just starting school learn four letter sounds (three consonants and a vowel), and then are shown words which are built up from those letter sounds. For example, in the space of a few days they will learn the letters 's', 'a', 't', 'p' and then when shown unfamiliar words, such as 'at', 'sat', 'pat', 'tap', 'nap', 'taps', 'pats', they can blend the letter sounds to find out what the words are. This gives children a lot of independence in reading from very early on and means that there need not be a partial alphabetic phase, where a child tries to read words by saying another word starting with the same letter such as saying 'toy' when the word is 'tap', or by getting the beginning and end letters, saying 'top' for 'tap'. They can start taking account of graphemes all through the word right from the start, within days of starting school. When faced with an unfamiliar word they have a strategy to work out what it is for themselves, so they do not need to look at the picture for cues, or try to guess what it is from the rest of the sentence. Once they have seen a word a few times and worked out what it is, they may recognise it on subsequent occasions without having to build up the pronunciation. This is a big advantage when reading for meaning, as a child can focus on getting meaning from the text, rather than expending a lot of effort on working out what the words are.

Research suggests that poor readers look like partial alphabetic readers (Romani et al., 2005), and there is evidence that very bright poor readers in particular take a rather visual approach to reading (Johnston and Morrison, 2007). This suggests that such children are not taking full advantage of the alphabetic code underlying English spelling. Given that with the synthetic phonics method there are very few underachievers (Johnston and Watson, 2005), it is likely that this method of teaching inhibits children at risk of reading failure from developing a partial alphabetic approach to reading that will in itself become a barrier to developing high levels of word recognition skill. Getting stuck with a partial alphabetic approach is not only bad for skilled automatised word recognition, it is also likely to lead to poor spelling ability.

A SUMMARY OF **KEY POINTS**

> The Primary National Strategy in England has adopted the Simple View of Reading. This model proposes that decoding printed words (D) is a separate skill which together with linguistic comprehension ability (C) gives a good account of a child's reading comprehension (R), that is $R = D \times C$.

> Children having problems with either decoding or linguistic comprehension will have problems with reading comprehension.

> To use the sounds of the letters of the alphabet to derive the pronunciation of words, children are taught phonics.

> In analytic phonics children learn to recognise words by sight and then learn about letter sounds at the beginning, at the end and then finally in the middle of words. It can take a year to start to learn to use letter sounds all through an unfamiliar word to find its pronunciation.

> In synthetic phonics, children learn to blend the letters sounds all through an unfamiliar word to get its pronunciation right from the start of reading tuition.

> Ehri's model of sight word reading development describes four phases in reading development: (1) pre-alphabetic, (2) partial alphabetic, (3) full alphabetic, and (4) consolidated alphabetic.

> When children learn to recognise words using a synthetic phonics method, they are developing a full alphabetic phase approach, bypassing the previous two phases.

Reflective task answers

Observing children showing the following patterns of reading, in which column would you place each child? Enter a number for each child. They may be in more than one phase, pick the most likely one.

1. Child reads 'Ribena' on the bottle but cannot read it in normal print.
2. Child reads 'kicking' without sounding and blending but has not seen this combination of morphemes ('kick' and 'ing') before.
3. Child reads 'Kit-Kat' on a packet and can sound and blend 'kitkat' when it is presented in normal print.
4. Child reads 'pill' for the word 'pail' – both words presented in normal print.

Pre-alphabetic	Partial alphabetic	Full alphabetic	Consolidated alphabetic
1	4	3	2

REFERENCES REFERENCES **REFERENCES** REFERENCES **REFERENCES** REFERENCES

Cain, K., and Oakhill, J. (2004). Reading comprehension difficulties in Nunes, T., and Bryant, P. (Eds.) *Handbook of Children's Literacy*. Dordrecht: Kluwer Academic.

Connelly, V., Johnston, R. S. and Thompson, G. B. (2001) The effects of phonics instruction on the reading comprehension of beginning readers. *Reading and Writing*, 14: 423–57.

Ehri, L. C. (1992) Reconceptualising the development of sight word reading and its relationship to recording, in Gough, P. B., Ehri, I. D., Treiman, R. (Eds), *Reading Acquisition*. Hillsdale, NJ: Erlbaum.

Ehri, L. C. (2004) Development of sight word reading: phases and findings, in Snowling, M. J. and Hulme, C. (Eds) *The Science of Reading: A Handbook*. Oxford: Blackwell, pp135–54.

Goodman, K. S. (1973) The 13th easy way to make learning to read difficult: a reaction to Gleitman and Rozin. *Reading Research Quarterly*, 8: 484–93.

Gough, P. B, and Tunmer W. E. (1986) Decoding, reading and reading disability. *Remedial Special Education*, 7: 6–10.

Hoover, W. A. and Gough, P. B. (1990) The Simple View of Reading. *Reading and Writing*, 2: 127–60.

Johnston, R. S., Anderson, M. and Holligan, C. (1996) Knowledge of the alphabet and explicit awareness of phonemes in pre-readers: the nature of the relationship. *Reading and Writing*, 8: 217–34.

Johnston, R. S. and Morrison, M. (2007) Towards a resolution of inconsistencies in the phonological deficit theory of reading disorders: phonological reading difficulties are more severe in high IQ poor readers. *Journal of Learning Disabilities*, 40: 66–79.

Johnston, R. S. and Thompson, G. B. (1989) Is dependence on phonological information in children's reading a product of instructional approach? *Journal of Experimental Child Psychology*, 48: 131–45.

Johnston, R. S. and Watson, J. (2004) Accelerating the development of reading, spelling and phonemic awareness. *Reading and Writing*, 17 (4): 327–57.

Johnston, R. S., and Watson, J. (2005) The effects of synthetic phonics teaching on reading and spelling attainment, a seven year longitudinal study. Scottish Executive Education Department. **www.scotland.gov.uk/library5/education/sptrs-00.asp**

Orton Dyslexia Society (1994) A new definition of dyslexia. *Bulletin of the Orton Dyslexia Society*, Fall.

Primary National Strategy (2006) The Primary Framework for literacy and mathematics: core position papers underpinning the renewal of guidance for literacy teaching and mathematics. **www.standards.dfes.gov.uk/primary/features/primary/pri_fwk_corepapers/**

Romani, C., Olson, A. and DiBetta, A. M. (2005) Spelling disorders, in Snowling, M. J. and Hulme, C. (Eds), *The Science of Reading: A Handbook.* Oxford: Blackwell, pp 431–47.

Smith, F. (1982) *Understanding reading.* New York: Holt, Rinehart and Winston.

Stanovich, K. (1980) Toward an interactive-compensatory model of individual differences in the development of reading fluency. *Reading Research Quarterly*, 16: 32–71.

Stuart, M. and Masterson, J. (1992) Patterns of reading and spelling in 10 year old children related to prereading phonological abilities. *Journal of Experimental Child Psychology*, 54: 168–87.

4
An introduction to *Letters and Sounds* and how to teach synthetic phonics

Learning objectives

In this chapter you will:

- **gain an understanding of the new Primary National Strategy Programme *Letters and Sounds*;**
- **learn how well this programme fits with our research and practice;**
- **see an overview of a typical synthetic phonic lesson;**
- **gain an understanding of the phases of phonic development outlined in *Letters and Sounds*.**

Those recommended for the award of Qualified Teacher Status (QTS) should meet the following Professional Standards:

Q12: Know a range of approaches to assessment, including the importance of formative assessment.

Q14: Have a secure knowledge and understanding of their subjects/curriculum areas and related pedagogy to enable them to teach effectively across the age and ability range for which they are trained.

Q15: Know and understand the relevant statutory and non-statutory curricula and frameworks, including those provided through the National Strategies, for their subjects/curriculum areas, and other relevant initiatives applicable to the age and ability range for which they are trained.

Q22: Plan for progression across the age and ability range for which they are trained, designing effective learning sequences within lessons and across series of lessons and demonstrating secure subject/curriculum knowledge.

Q26:

   (a) Make effective use of a range of assessment, monitoring and recording strategies.

   (b) Assess the learning needs of those they teach in order to set challenging learning objectives.

Q27: Provide timely, accurate and constructive feedback on learners' attainment, progress and areas for development.

Q28: Support and guide learners to reflect on their learning, identify the progress they have made and identify their emerging learning needs.

Q29: Evaluate the impact of their teaching on the progress of all learners, and modify their planning and classroom practice where necessary.

Overview of *Letters and Sounds*

The Primary National Strategy programme *Letters and Sounds* (DfES, 2007) is a synthetic phonics scheme that replaces *Progression in Phonics* and *Playing with Sounds*. It is very different from the previous programmes in many respects. By and large, it does not build on what went before, it is a different type of phonics.

A major difference is that *Letters and Sounds* adopts the Simple View of Reading (see Chapter 3), which identifies two processes in reading comprehension – recognising words and comprehending text. The *Notes of Guidance* section of *Letters and Sounds* states that in the early days of learning to read children need to learn how to recognise printed words. Once they have acquired some decoding skill, children can make sense of simple written sentences using the same processes that they use to understand spoken language. When children can recognise and spell words with ease, they will be able to concentrate on understanding what they read and produce good written work. The role of synthetic phonics teaching, therefore, is to establish children's word recognition and spelling skills early on in their schooling, as a basis for developing good reading comprehension and writing skills.

Letters and Sounds: Notes of Guidance specifically states that children should not use unreliable strategies when dealing with unfamiliar words, such as looking at pictures or looking at the first sound, and then guessing the word. These approaches were commonly used alongside *Progression in Phonics* and *Playing with Sounds,* but these strategies encourage a primitive sight-word approach to reading not well underpinned by letter-sound information. This approach is very undesirable, not the least because individuals with a reading disability often find it very hard to break out of this way of dealing with the printed word (Johnston, 1985).

Letters and Sounds also makes it clear that invented spellings should be corrected sensitively, so that children do not learn the wrong spellings. One of us had a 12 year old pupil with literacy problems who spelt the word 'said' as 'siad' every time, and found it hard to break out of the habit, as this spelling looked correct to him. A boy in the same class whose name was Lawrie, spelt it as Larwie every time he wrote his name!

Learning about letters

According to *Letters and Sounds* children should:

- learn to distinguish letter shapes from other letter shapes;
- learn to associate letter shapes with sounds, and vice versa;
- learn letter formation;
- learn to associate letter shapes with names, and vice versa.

In synthetic phonics programmes, letters and sounds (or more accurately, grapheme-to-phoneme correspondences) are taught as a defined incremental sequence. In *Letters and Sounds*, as each new grapheme is taught, children blend for reading and segment for spelling using both the new and the previously taught graphemes. This is quite different to *Progression in Phonics*, where children learnt letter sounds at the beginning of words, then at the end, and finally in the middle, and only then started to sound and blend to read words. In our studies we have found sounding and blending for reading was introduced for most children at the start of Year 1 when *Progression in Phonics* was used (Primary 2 in Scotland).

Letters and Sounds gives a lot of guidance on how to teach letters; the key idea here is that letter learning should be multi-sensory. This means that letter formation should be taught right from the start; as children learn a letter sound, they also learn to form it in the air, and then on a whiteboard or piece of paper. Learning the visual appearance, the writing move-ment and the sound of a letter, all at the same time, helps them to consolidate it in memory. *Letters and Sounds* also recommends children use magnetic boards in pairs, to reinforce work done by the teacher on a large magnetic board. This sort of multi-sensory approach is very effective, and mirrors what we did in the programme we used in Clackmannanshire. Some synthetic phonics schemes also use mnemonics to help children learn the letter sounds. These mnemonics might involve associating a letter with a character whose name starts with that sound, e.g. the letter 'j' might be represented by a character called Jim. Other approaches involve hand actions and distinctive sounds. *Letters and Sounds: Notes of Guidance* says that mnemonics have proved beneficial in helping chil-dren remember letters. However, it also says that teachers should take care that children understand that the mnemonic and multi-sensory activities (such as drawing, painting, making models, and becoming involved in stories) carried out for reinforcing letter learn-ing are not an end in themselves. Children need to stay focussed on the role of letters in reading and spelling words.

Another issue covered by *Letters and Sounds: Notes of Guidance* is when to introduce letter names; it points out that they will be needed by the start of Phase 3. You will find that it is difficult to teach about vowel digraphs without using letter names. It is problematical to say (using the letter sounds) that /a/ and /i/ together sound /ai/ as in 'bait'. Early on in our studies, we first introduced letter names when we got to the point of teaching vowel and consonant digraphs (e.g. 'ai', 'th'). However, synthetic phonics is taught so rapidly that we soon realised that it makes sense to teach the letter names before the programme starts. Children often know an alphabet song from nursery, so it is easy to use the song they already know whilst showing them a visual representation of the letters.

How are high-frequency words dealt with?

It has been common practice in schools to treat high-frequency words as 'sight recognition words', even when these words are phonically decodable (by 'decodable' we mean words that can be sounded and blended for reading). However, it is not clear that it was ever the intention of the authors of the previous Primary National Strategy programmes that high frequency words should be taught without attention to letter-sound information. Indeed, on page 7 of *Progression in Phonics* (DfEE, 1999) it says that *The high frequency words listed in the back of the Framework are not intended to be taught by rote*. A sight or rote approach with decodable words is undesirable in a synthetic phonic programme, as the aim of the teaching is for children to recognise words by a mature form of sight-word reading well underpinned by letter-sound information. Any teaching using flash cards, where the children are expected to read words visually, seriously undermines the synthetic phonics method. Furthermore, many of the words which are of high frequency in children's books will rapidly become fully decodable, as the synthetic phonics method is so accelerated. Indeed, accord-ing to the Core Position Papers (Primary National Strategy, 2006), Phases 2 and 3 of *Letters and Sounds* should take only a maximum of 18 weeks to complete. This means that children will be able to decode many high-frequency words soon after starting school.

This leaves the problem of irregularly spelt words. *Letters and Sounds: Notes of Guidance* recommends that children should be encouraged to focus on the pronounceable elements of these 'tricky' words. The approach we took in our research was similarly to show children that there is always some guide to pronunciation in these words. Even the word 'yacht', the spelling of which comes from Dutch, has a first and last letter which gives a guide to pronunciation. We sometimes used to spell the word as 'yott', so it is not clear why the Dutch-influenced spelling 'yacht' caught on; possibly at one time it did represent how we spoke the word.

Reading text

There is a commonly-held belief that synthetic phonics necessarily involves a late start to reading text. *Letters and Sounds* recommends an early start to reading decodable text, firstly through caption reading and then through sentences. Similarly, in our studies, the children read captions as soon as they had learnt three or four letters. For example, after teaching 's' 'a' 't' 'p', the children could read 'a tap', 'Pat at a tap', 'Pat sat a tap'. As more and more letters were learnt, the children increasingly read fully formed sentences. The children also started using reading scheme books about six weeks after the synthetic phonics programme began. These books were not 'decodable' readers, but the phonics teaching was very effective without this resource; the teachers prepared the children beforehand for any words that were not fully decodable. However, many publishers are introducing decodable readers now, so you may find these helpful to use alongside your synthetic phonics scheme.

Fidelity to the programme

Letters and Sounds: Notes of Guidance makes it very clear that once you have selected the synthetic phonics programme you are going to use, you should follow it consistently. This is not a situation in which you can cherry pick the parts that appeal to you; these programmes have a tried and tested sequence that optimally develops children's phonic skills. This is analogous to maths teaching, where sticking to the progression worked out by the programme's authors leads to the most effective learning by the children. Learning to decode the printed word is a similarly technical matter, but there will be plenty of opportunities in the language area of the curriculum for you to show your creativity as a teacher!

A typical synthetic phonics lesson

Letters and Sounds: Six-phase Teaching Programme gives a great deal of guidance on what synthetic phonics lessons should include, and how to implement the various elements, but the suggested lesson structure varies between and within phases, so it is difficult to show a typical lesson. In our programme, however, we have found we can keep the same lesson structure throughout. Table 4.1 shows what a typical synthetic phonics lesson could look like (we will look in detail at how to teach a typical synthetic phonics lesson in Chapter 6).

Table 4.1 A typical synthetic phonics lesson for learning a new grapheme

Introduction	The children sing an alphabet song, looking at the appropriate letter as each name is sung.
Revision	There is quick-fire practice of previously taught graphemes and phonemes, then there is practice of reading, letter formation and spelling using these graphemes and phonemes.
Lesson	The teacher speaks about the learning intentions and outcomes for the day. The new grapheme for the day is then introduced, and its sound is given. The children search for this new letter in printed words and say whether it comes up in the initial, middle or final position of words, which encourages a left-to-right visual search strategy.

Using the new grapheme together with previously taught ones, the children sound and blend printed words for reading, segment spoken words for spelling, and practise writing the new grapheme. Early on spelling is mostly done with children using magnetic letters on boards, either individually or in pairs.

Apply Here the children read or write captions and sentences using tricky words and words made up from the taught graphemes

Follow-up Follow-up activities include searching for the new letter or grapheme in words, and practising letter formation.

The learning outcomes are discussed, and then the children sing the alphabet song again.

Our approach actually differs slightly from this in our studies. Instead of having an 'Apply' section in the daily lesson, as in *Letters and Sounds*, we have lessons for consolidation that come after a few grapheme-phoneme learning lessons have been carried out. In these lessons children read and spell irregular words, and practise the reading, spelling and writing of captions made up from the previously taught letters. For learning letter identification, *Letters and Sounds* recommends that the children use letter fans to display a set of letters; they hear a letter sound and then search for the corresponding letter. In our lessons (see the 'Lesson' section in Table 4.1 above) the children search for the target letter in actual words; this is designed to reinforce the idea that words should be scanned from left to right, as well as to improve letter recognition. These are very minor differences. Although the *Letters and Sounds* programme has not been tested experimentally in classes as our programme has, it so closely follows ours that we are confident that if you follow the procedures it outlines, your children will make a very good start in learning to read. One proviso is that the effects of the play-like approach described in *Letters and Sounds* have not been tested experimentally. The caution given in *Letters and Sounds* about the use of mnemonics in letter learning also applies here – it is important to be sure that the children are focussing on the phonic goal of the activity, and not on the play element itself.

Teachers will need to do a considerable amount of preparation to use *Letters and Sounds*. The lesson plans advocated in *Letters and Sounds* (see below) show it to be a highly structured method of teaching. Daily lessons will need to be produced using the suggested letter order and the word banks of regular and irregular (tricky) words. If you are new to teaching, or even if you are not, you might find it easier to use a commercial programme that meets the Primary National Strategy's criteria. You should be able to find one containing fully detailed daily lesson plans, as well as electronic and photocopiable resources to support those lessons. You will also find that some commercial programmes provide formative and summative assessments along the lines recommended in *Letters and Sounds*.

Assessment

In order to teach effectively it is important to know how well the children are doing, and this may not be apparent just through observation. *Letters and Sounds* recommends reliable individual assessment of children's learning as they move through the phases. The skills to be assessed are summarised phase by phase in Appendix 3 of *Letters and Sounds*. In summary, children should be able to:

- give the phonemes to all or most of the taught graphemes;
- find those graphemes when given the phonemes;
- write the letters for the graphemes;
- blend to read words made up from the taught phonemes;
- segment a spoken word and make a phonemically plausible attempt to spell it;
- read the taught 'tricky' (or irregular) words.

The level of skill required for the last three here in particular increases across the phases. You can read more about how to diagnose the problems of slow learners in Chapter 7, where we describe assessments appropriate to the phases. We also give an example of how such assessments were used to plan the learning support programme of a child with special educational needs.

Ability group versus whole class teaching

Letters and Sounds gives no advice on whether children should be taught in small groups according to ability, or on a whole class basis. When you read about assessment in *Letters and Sounds* you may conclude that children must have complete mastery of what they have been taught before continuing with the programme, which implies that some groups should move at a slower pace. In our study in Clackmannanshire, the children were taught on a whole class basis for 16 weeks, and this proved to be very beneficial for the slower learners. They were constantly exposed to new print vocabulary, and to the processes of blending and segmenting, and were able to see what the goals of the programme were. They would not have achieved these benefits if they had proceeded at a very much slower pace than the other groups in the class. The teachers in Clackmannanshire found they were also able to keep the class together for phonics lessons throughout the second year of school. There were unexpected benefits of whole class teaching – a school inspector told us he had observed in one of our study schools that the children had better self-esteem, and that there were fewer problems in the playground.

We recommend from our experience that children who are slow to learn the letter sounds, and to blend and segment, do well if they get extra practice in a 'nurture' group at some other time during the day, staying with their classmates for the phonics lessons rather than working through the programme more slowly. This may sound surprising, but the low level of underachievement we found in our study in Clackmannanshire (see Chapter 1) shows that keeping all of the children together in the class programme is very effective. Slowing down the programme for some slower learning children may be setting them up for reading failure; they may never catch up with their classmates, however much extra practice in reading they get.

Overview of phases

The *Letter and Sounds* programme is split into six phases. These phases are outlined in *The Primary Framework for Literacy and Mathematics* (Primary National Strategy, 2006). *Letters and Sounds: Notes of Guidance* makes it very clear that the boundaries between the phases are not fixed. Phonics starts in Phase 2. Phase 1 prepares for Phase 2, and has activities designed to develop children's oral blending and segmenting of the sounds in spoken words, as well as speaking and listening skills. However, it is made clear in *Letters and Sounds: Notes of Guidance* that children do not need to complete all seven aspects of the Phase 1 programme before starting Phase 2, and indeed Phase 1 work can run alongside

Phase 2 work. This view is supported by our research (see Chapter 1), which showed that children who started with no awareness of phonemes, and an inability to produce even one rhyming word, nevertheless made very good progress with synthetic phonics. This is because the fundamental skills of blending and segmenting are very much easier to teach through the medium of letters and print than through purely oral activities. The visual information from print makes blending and segmenting less abstract and more meaningful.

The phases are a convenient way of showing the progression that children's learning will take.

Phase 1

This work is to be carried out in the Early Years Foundation Stage. It is not part of the phonic programme, but prepares children for phonic work. The activities are designed to get children to listen and to discriminate between sounds. The activities are arranged under seven aspects.

1. General sound discrimination – environmental sounds.
2. General sound discrimination – instrumental sounds.
3. General sound discrimination – body percussion.
4. Rhythm and rhyme.
5. Alliteration.
6. Voice sounds.
7. Oral blending and segmenting.

In Appendix 3 we have included a daily programme of lessons that we have used in schools, which covers Aspect 7: Oral blending and segmenting.

We have found in our research that there are other skills that can usefully be taught before Phase 2 starts, such as the conventions of print, the vocabulary of reading, and learning letter names. Much of this can be done when reading stories with the children. You can discuss:

- **the left-to-right and top-to bottom directionality of print;**
- **that words are made up of letters, and that spaces are used between words;**
- **the use of lower and upper case letters and punctuation;**
- **positional words such as page, top, bottom, beginning, end, first, middle, last, right, left;**
- **you can also teach an Alphabet Song, which the children sing while the letters on the board are pointed out.**

Phase 2

The basic lesson plan in *Letters and Sounds* is as follows:

Introduction:	Objectives and criteria for success.
Revisit and Review:	Practise previously learned letters.
	Practise oral blending and segmentation.
Teach:	Teach a new letter.
	Teach blending and/or segmentation with letters (weeks 2 and 3).
	Teach one or two 'tricky' words (week 3 onwards).
Practise:	Practise reading and/or spelling words with the new letter.

Apply: Read or write a caption (with the teacher) using one or more high-frequency words and words containing the new letter (week 3 onwards.

Assess: Learning against criteria.

This phase starts in Reception (Primary 1 in Scotland); the duration is intended to be up to six weeks, in which time 19 letters are taught. To start with, children learn about the visual appearance, the sounds, and the formation of the letters s, a, t, p, i, n. Synthetic phonics gets going when five or six letter sounds have been taught, in the second week of Phase 2 – that is, once children have learnt a few consonants and at least one vowel, they can begin sounding and blending for reading, and segmenting for spelling, building on the oral blending and segmenting that they have been carrying out in Phase 1.

Sounding and blending

In blending for reading, the child sees a printed word she does not know, converts the letters into sounds from left to right, and then blends these sounds together to find out what the word is. An example is as follows.

The child sees the word 'pat', but cannot instantly recognise it. However, she knows the letter sounds for 'p', 'a', and 't'. She says these sounds from left to right, and then blends them together to find out that the word is 'pat'.

REFLECTIVE TASK

Here is a made-up word – 'pralimtoren'. Using the letter sounds see what you come up with as you blend the sounds from left to right. Given your level of reading skill you may not need to do this letter by letter.

Segmenting for spelling

In segmenting for spelling the child hears the word, breaks it down into its constituent sounds, and then maps these sounds onto the letters. Segmenting for spelling is not traditionally part of synthetic phonics, but it is a very helpful development of the method as it promotes phonemic awareness and a systematic approach to spelling. See the following example.

The child hears the word 'sat'. She says the word, works out the first sound is /s/, and pulls down the letter 's' on her magnetic board. She says the word again, and hears that the middle one is /a/, and pulls down the letter 'a'. Then she says the word again, and hears that the final sound is /t/. She pulls down the letter 't'.

She now has 's a t' on her board. She blends these letter sounds together to check she has the letters in the right order.

Letter formation

Children learn to write the letters at the same time as learning the sounds in *Letters and Sounds*, forming them in the air, on a whiteboard, and on paper using pencils. However, they can do their *spelling* using magnetic letters on a board until they have the physical co-ordination necessary for writing the letters with a pencil.

Summary of Phase 2

The key idea here is that children understand that blending and segmenting are reversible processes. Using sounding and blending for reading, and segmenting for spelling, children soon read and spell simple VC and CVC words, such as 'at', 'sat' and 'pat'. The children read and spell more and more new words as each letter sound is taught. They will learn that some words are 'tricky', either because they have irregular spellings, or because they are not yet decodable, but these will not be taught purely as sight words. They will also learn to read some two-syllable words.

Phase 3

The basic lesson plan in *Letters and Sounds* is as follows:

Introduction:	Objectives and criteria for success.
Revisit and Review:	Practise previously learned letters or graphemes.
Teach:	Teach new graphemes. Teach one or two tricky words.
Practise:	Practise blending and reading words with a new GPC *(i.e. grapheme to phoneme correspondence)*. Practise segmenting and spelling words with a new GPC.
Apply:	Read or write a caption or a sentence using one or more tricky-words and words containing the graphemes.
Assess:	Learning against criteria.

This phase is intended to last for up to 12 weeks. A major difference from Phase 2 is that the children now learn that some sounds in our language are spelt by more than one letter, e.g. the consonant digraph 'sh' as in 'shop', the vowel digraph 'oa' as in 'boat'. However, children are *not* taught that the 'oa' sound can also be spelt as 'note'; this introduction to the variability of spelling in English comes in Phase 5. Altogether, 25 new graphemes are taught in this phase, made up of the remaining letters of the alphabet, and some vowel and consonant digraphs. By the end of this phase the children will have learned to read and spell using one grapheme for each of the 43 phonemes. (These phonemes are shown in a table on page 11 of *Letters and Sounds: Notes of Guidance*.) Many of the consonant phonemes are shown in the initial position of words, for ease of presentation for teachers. However, letter sounds are taught all through the word in synthetic phonics, so the example of /m/ – map could easily have been shown as /m/ – 'ham'.

Phase 4

The basic lesson plan in *Letters and Sounds* is as follows:

Introduction:	Objectives and criteria for success.
Revisit and Review:	Practise previously learned graphemes.
Teach:	Teach blending and segmentation of adjacent consonants. Teach some tricky words.
Practise:	Practise blending and reading words with adjacent consonants. Practise segmentation and spelling words with adjacent consonants.

| Apply: | Read or write sentences using one or more high-frequency words and words containing adjacent consonants. |
| Assess: | Learning against criteria. |

The typical duration of this phase is four to six weeks. Here children learn about adjacent consonants, e.g. 'slip', 'ca<u>mp</u>'. Most synthetic phonics schemes introduce this much earlier, generally once all the single letter sounds have been taught. This is because reading words with adjacent consonants comes very easily to children who can sound and blend. Indeed, *Letters and Sounds: Notes of Guidance* specifically points out that many children will be capable of taking this step much earlier than Phase 4. In our study in Clackmannanshire, we successfully taught the reading and spelling of words with adjacent consonants from just a few weeks into the programme. The late introduction of adjacent consonants in *Letters and Sounds* is probably a carry over from analytic phonics, where such items were taught in word families, e.g. 'slip', '<u>slot</u>'. However, it should be stressed that children should not be taught families of words in this way. Our studies have shown that this approach can impede the progress of slower learning children. It is expected that Phase 4 teaching will be completed before the end of Reception (Primary 1); Phases 2 to 4 should take a maximum of 24 weeks teaching to complete.

Phase 5

The basic lesson plan in *Letters and Sounds* is as follows:

Introduction:	Objectives and criteria for success.
Revisit and Review:	Practise previously learned graphemes.
	Practise blending and segmentation.
Teach:	Teach new graphemes.
	Teach tricky words.
Practise:	Practise blending and reading words with the new GPC *(i.e. grapheme to phoneme correspondences)*.
	Practise segmenting and spelling words with the new GPC.
Apply:	Read or write a sentence using one or more high-frequency words and words containing the new graphemes.
Assess:	Learning against criteria.

Phase 5 extends through Year 1 (Primary 2 in Scotland). Up to this point, the children have generally learnt one grapheme for each of the sounds in spoken English. They will have read some words with more than one syllable, some words with vowel and consonant digraphs, and also words with adjacent consonants. At this point they will start to learn that some spellings have alternative pronunciations, e.g. 'c<u>ow</u>', 'bl<u>ow</u>', and some sounds have alternative spellings, e.g. '<u>j</u>ump', 'he<u>dge</u>'. There are some phonic rules to guide children here, for example in how to spell the /j/ sound at the end of a word, but out of necessity some word-specific spellings will need to be learnt.

Phase 6

Letters and Sounds does not suggest a lesson plan for this phase, but we have found it possible to use the lesson plan we outlined in Table 4.1, pages 37–8. This phase begins in and continues through Year 2 (Primary 3 in Scotland). By now most children should be able to recognise a large number of words without sounding and blending them; that is, they should show fluency and automaticity in reading familiar words. However, they will still need to sound and blend unfamiliar words. A lot of the teaching in this phase revolves around spelling, as it is harder to develop than reading, but this will have pay-offs for reading. When we add prefixes, e.g. 'return', and suffixes, e.g. 'sitting', we are adding grammatical morphemes to root morphemes (such as 'turn' and 'sit') that children know very well. Children's reading will become more fluent if they recognise these familiar chunks, and thus sound and blend them at the syllable level, e.g. re/place. This awareness of the grammatical morphemes will develop as you teach children the spelling rules for adding them on to base words. For example, where there is a long vowel sound, e.g. 'hope', the 'e' that lengthened the vowel sound is taken off, and –ing is added, forming 'hoping'. However, words with short vowel sounds, e.g. 'hop', have their last letter doubled up, e.g. 'hopping'. Discrete phonics teaching continues, with children learning about the less common grapheme to phoneme correspondences, and also about phonic irregularities. Some spellings are word specific and just have to be learnt; if you are in any doubt about the variability of English vowel spelling, have a look at these words: due/zoo/blew/you!

A SUMMARY OF **KEY POINTS**

> **Sounding and blending is the primary means by which children should attempt to read unfamiliar words (they should not guess from pictures or context).**

> **The reverse process is segmenting for spelling (invented spellings should be sensitively corrected).**

> **As each letter sound is taught, the children should learn how to form the letter.**

> **Children should read high-frequency words and tricky (i.e. irregular) words using letter-sound information as far as possible.**

> **Children should start to read captions and sentences as soon as possible.**

> **Assess your pupils' learning to see if they have learnt the grapheme to phoneme associations you have taught, and if they can use them to sound and blend for reading and segment for spelling.**

> **We recommend that slow learners stay in the class programme, but do catch-up activities at other times during the day.**

> **Fidelity to the programme you have selected is essential, do not cherry pick from it.**

> *Letters and Sounds* **has six phases, with Phases 2 to 6 covering phonics. As the children progress through the phonics phases, children learn to read and spell:**
  – **simple CVC words, like 'sat';**
  – **words with consonant and vowel digraphs, like 'shop', 'coat';**
  – **words with adjacent consonants, like 'slip', 'camp';**
  – **vowel digraphs with variable pronunciations, like 'cow', 'blow';**
  – **consonants and vowels with alternative spellings, e.g. 'jump', 'hedge';**
  – **words with prefixes and suffixes, e.g. 'return', 'sitting';**
  – **rules for adding suffixes, like 'hope'→ 'hoping', 'hop'→ 'hopping'.**

REFERENCES REFERENCES **REFERENCES** REFERENCES **REFERENCES** REFERENCES

DfEE (1999) *Progression in Phonics*. London: DfEE.
www.standards.dfes.gov.uk/primary/publications/lieracy/63309/

DfES (2007) *Letters and Sounds.* London: DfES. **www.standards.dfes.gov.uk/local/clld/las.html**

Johnston, P. H. (1985) Understanding reading disability: a case study approach. *Harvard Educational Review*, 55: 153–77.

Primary National Strategy (2006) The Primary Framework for Literacy and Mathematics: Guidance for practitioners and teachers on progression and pace in the teaching of phonics (Annex B Outline of Progression). **www.standards.dfes.gov.uk/primary/features/primary/pri_fwk_corepapers/**

5
How do I start to teach synthetic phonics?

Learning objectives

In this chapter you will learn how to:

- **start to teach the basic skills for synthetic phonics;**
- **help your children to acquire alphabet knowledge;**
- **introduce children to letter sounds and letter formation;**
- **blend (synthesise) letter sounds together to read words;**
- **break up (segment) the sounds in words to spell;**
- **teach your children the procedures for blending and segmenting;**
- **evaluate your children's learning regularly for formative/diagnostic assessment purposes.**

Those recommended for the award of Qualified Teacher Status (QTS) should meet the following Professional Standards.

Q12: Know a range of approaches to assessment, including the importance of formative assessment.

Q22: Plan for progression across the age and ability range for which they are trained, designing effective learning sequences within lessons and across series of lessons and demonstrating secure subject/curriculum knowledge.

Q25: Teach lessons and sequences of lessons across the age and ability range for which they are trained in which they:

(a) use a range of strategies and resources including e-learning taking practical account of diversity and promoting equality and inclusion;

(b) build on prior knowledge, develop concepts and processes, enable learners to apply new knowledge, understanding and skills and meet learning objectives;

(c) adapt their language to suit the learners they teach, introducing new ideas and concepts clearly and using explanations, questions, discussions and plenaries effectively;

(d) demonstrate the ability to manage the learning of individuals, groups and whole classes, modifying their teaching to suit the stage of the lesson.

Q26:

(a) Make effective use of a range of assessment, monitoring and recording strategies;

(b) Assess the learning needs of those they teach in order to set challenging learning objectives.

Q27: Provide timely, accurate and constructive feedback on learners' attainment, progress and areas of development.

Q28: Support and guide learners to reflect on their learning, identify the progress they have made and identify their emerging learning needs.

Q29: Evaluate the impact of their teaching on the progress of all learners and modify their planning and classroom practice where necessary.

Introduction

How do I start to teach synthetic phonics?

In addressing this question, we will describe the planning and philosophy underlying the use of systematic synthetic phonics (which includes segmenting words for spelling). It is a balanced approach integrating reading, writing, spelling and phonemic awareness, coupled with relevant language activities (Watson and Johnston, 2000). In this chapter we will show you how to do a lesson that follows the recommendations made in *Letters and Sounds* (DfES, 2007). Where relevant, compliance with recommendations in the Rose Review (2006) will be indicated.

Our writing system is alphabetic and the Rose Review points out that *all beginner readers have to come to terms with the alphabetic principles if they are to learn to read and write* (2006, para. 34). The letters of the alphabet (graphemes) represent the speech sounds of the language (phonemes) and children need to learn that letters must be connected to their sounds in order to pronounce unfamiliar printed words (Watson and Johnston, 2000).

In this and the following chapter, we will explain not only how to develop your children's knowledge of letter sound correspondences but also how they learn to use this knowledge to sound and blend for reading and to segment for spelling. We will describe how to teach the various *elements* of a synthetic phonics programme in this chapter, and then in Chapter 6 we will explain how to integrate all of these basic elements into a specific *lesson*.

Overview of chapter

Getting started: teaching the basic skills

(A) Teaching the alphabet – letter names, letter sounds and letter formation.
(B) Teaching blending for word reading and segmenting for spelling.
(C) Formative/diagnostic assessment.
(D) Overview of basis skills acquisition procedures.

(A) Teaching the alphabet – letter names, letter sounds and letter formation

In our research in schools (Watson, 1998), we found that the teaching of letter sounds preceded the teaching of letter names. In fact, in many cases letter names were not taught until Year 1 (Primary 2). For many years it had been thought that it was confusing for children to learn both together (Rose Review, 2006). However, as letters of the alphabet are known by their letter names (and in certain instances the sound of a vowel digraph, e.g. 'ai' is the letter name /ai/), it is logical to teach both letter names and letter sounds together. The Rose Review proposes that it is *sensible to teach both names and sounds of letters* (2006, para. 81). The pronunciations of many of the letter names actually provide a clue to the letter sounds (see Table 5.1 below).

Table 5.1 Letters where the names give clues to the sounds of the letter

name	sound	name	sound
bee	/b/	eff	/f/
dee	/d/	ell	/l/
jay	/j/	em	/m/
kay	/k/	en	/n/
pea	/p/	ar	/r/
tea	/t/	ess	/s/
vee	/v/	ex	/x/
zed	/z/		

(i) Letter names taught via the alphabet song

In our studies, the letters of the alphabet were initially taught through an alphabet song where the children learnt to associate the letter names with upper and lower case magnetic letters in alphabetic order (Watson and Johnston, 2000). The following diagram sets out the procedure for helping children acquire such alphabet knowledge. The resources needed are as follows:

- a CD player and CD accompaniment for the alphabet song being used;
- a magnetic teaching board/wedge;
- lower and upper case magnetic letters of the alphabet.

The following diagram demonstrates the sequence for helping children to acquire alphabet knowledge.

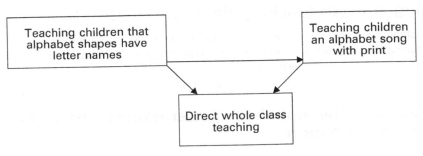

Figure 5.1 Helping children to acquire alphabet knowledge

The music for *Twinkle, Twinkle, Little Star* fits well with the words of the alphabet song shown below. The children learn to sing the letter names while the appropriate letters on the magnetic alphabet array are simultaneously pointed out. If the accompaniment is transferred to a CD, that will leave you free for teaching the children.

To fit in with the music, there is a short introductory section ('Come and listen, listen to me, etc', see below). It is also useful to have a short musical introduction on your CD to serve as a signal to the children that the alphabet activity is about to begin.

Words for *Twinkle Twinkle Little Star*	→	Words for the alphabet song
Twinkle, twinkle little star	→	Come and listen, listen to me
How I wonder what you are	→	Listen to my a b c
Up above the world so high	→	a b c d e f g
Like a diamond in the sky	→	h i j k lmn o p
Twinkle, twinkle little star	→	q r s t u v
How I wonder what you are.	→	w..... x y [&] z.

Teaching procedure with the whole class

To teach the alphabet song, match the words and syllables of the letter names to the rhythm of the song. Model the singing, pointing to the letters and encouraging the children to join in. Concentrate on one section at a time and gradually the children will be confident and keen to take part in the singing.

The children can practise the alphabet song daily, taking turns to point to the lower case letters, and then the upper case letters, while singing the letter names. In the electronic version of *Fast Phonics First* (Watson and Johnston, 2007), which is based on the programme we used in Clackmannanshire, both the lower case and upper case alphabets are available and the letters are automatically highlighted as the accompaniment is played. The accompaniment can also be clicked off for the children to sing by themselves. We include capital letters because they:

- provide a way of reinforcing the knowledge that the letter names refer to both lower and upper case letters;
- reinforce the fact that when the children come to learn the letter sounds, they also share the same sound (Watson and Johnston, 2000);
- accelerate the teaching of a sentence – as children know their names start with a capital letter it is only one step further to demonstrate how a capital letter is needed to start a sentence and finish it with a full stop, or indeed an exclamation mark or a question mark.

REFLECTIVE TASK

Task 1
Letter names of the alphabet
List what you think the children will learn from singing the alphabet song with print every day, using both lower and upper case letters. (Answers at the end of the chapter.)

ii) Introducing letter sounds and letter formation

We found that the children learnt the alphabet well using the teaching sequence of letter shapes, followed by letter names and finally letter sounds.

Before the children can start a synthetic phonics programme, four letter sounds need to be taught in isolation, one at a time (Watson and Johnston, 2000). How each of these letter sounds is taught is described below. When we put a letter in quotation marks, we are indicating the letter name, i.e. 's'. When we put the letter between forward slashes, we are indicating the letter sound i.e. /s/. Procedures for teaching /s/ on the first day are initially described in detail, and the same procedures are repeated on the following three days for the sounds /a/ /t/ and /p/ (that is, three consonants and one vowel). The sequence for teaching these sounds, which are the first four letters in *Letters and Sounds* (DfES, 2007), is displayed in the following diagram.

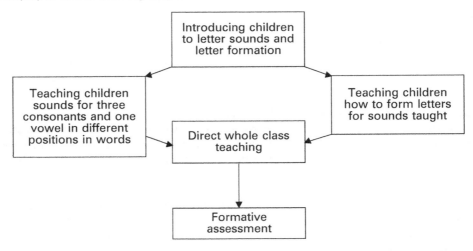

Figure 5.2 Teaching the initial small cluster of sounds together with letter formation

The first four letters in *Letters and Sounds* (DfES, 2007) are **s**, **a**, **t** and **p**. Table 5.2 illustrates how to teach children the sound and letter formation for the first letter 's' and the required resources.

Table 5.2 Teaching children the sound and letter formation procedure for 's'

What we want the children to be able to do	The resources which will be needed
Say the letter name you point out – 's' **Say** 's' sounds /s/; repeat this 's' sounds /s/ **Point out** the letter which sounds /s/ **Say** the sound for the printed letter – /s/ /s/ /s/ Say the sound for the letter written on the board	Magnetic alphabet for the teacher to point out the letter **s** Magnetic alphabet for children to point out **s** Card with the letter **s** in print **s** written on the board
Find the letter for the /s/ sound in letter sequences or words **Say** letter position, i.e. at the beginning, in the middle or at the end of each word	Four cards for letters **z e s x** (If following *Letters and Sounds*, a fan with the letters s a t p i n) Four cards for words **pants, Stan, past, spins**
Form the letter 's' following the description given by the teacher **Tell** the teacher how to write the letter 's' on the board	Magnetic letters for **s**, whiteboards and black felt pens Tray with damp sand, paper and pencil Board and chalk or whiteboard and black felt pen
Talk about what they have learnt	The above lesson plan as an aide memoire

Note the reversibility aspect of what we want the children to be able to do. Children can

- **find the correct letter when given the sound in letter sequences and words**
- **say the correct sound when shown the letter – in magnetic form, in print and written form**
- **form the letter correctly using a procedural description from the teacher**
- **tell the teacher how to write the letter on the board.**

Teaching procedure for day 1

Display the magnetic alphabet on the teaching magnetic board as below. Sing the alphabet song indicating each letter, lower case then upper case.

A B C D E F G H I J K L M N O P Q R S T U V W X Y Z
a b c d e f g h i j k l m n o p q r s t u v w x y z
▲

Teaching the letter sound

Point to the magnetic letter **s** (see arrow above), asking the children its name, then saying **'s'** **sounds** /s/. Repeat the sound with the children, then let the children say the sound /s/ on their own. Show the card with **s** printed on it on its own, then ask the children to say the sound. They should say **'s' sounds** /s/. Write the letter **s** on the board asking the children to say the sound again **'s' sounds** /s/.

Searching for the letter 's' in a letter sequence

Replace the letter **s** in the magnetic alphabet array, pull down the letters **z e s x**, and ask the children to point to the letter which sounds /s/. Replace these letters. Repeat the procedure using the pack of cards with the printed individual letters. Display the cards, asking the children to select the card with the letter for the sound /s/. Repeat the procedure, this time writing the four letters on the board and asking the children which one is /s/.

Searching for letters in letters sequences (*Letters and Sounds*)

An alternative approach is to arrange the letters **s, a, t, p, i, n** in a fan; the child hears the sound /s/, finds the letter for the sound /s/, leaves it at the top, and slides the other letters out of sight.

Searching for letters in words (see Table 5.2 on page 50)

Write on the board the four words **pants, Stan, past, spins**. Ask the children to find the letter for the sound /s/ in each of the words, saying whether it is at the beginning, in the middle or at the end of the word. Repeat this visual search showing the words on cards, the children pointing to the letter for the sound /s/ in each word, saying the position. Return to the words on the board asking the children to draw a circle round the letter for the sound /s/ in each word. (Note that the purpose of these words is for visually identifying the position of the target letter sound in words. Children are not being asked to try to read them.)

Our reason for asking children to identify the position of the target letter sound in *words,* as well as in a set of letters (as recommended in *Letters and Sounds*), is to encourage them to think of the words as an ordered sequence of letters. They need to learn to examine the words in a left-to-right direction and use the correct vocabulary for saying where the letter sound is positioned (Watson and Johnston, 2000).

(iii) Teaching children how to form letters for the taught sounds

Using the magnetic letter **s**, demonstrate how to follow round the shape with your finger saying where and how to start, follow the shape round and back and where to stop. Repeat this procedure with the children carrying out the movement from your description with their own magnetic letter **s**, experiencing the shape through using their fingers. Repeat this procedure again with the children joining in with your movement 'jingle'.

Ask the children to place their magnetic **s** letter on the desk beside them and form the letter '**s**' on top of the desk using their fingers as you and the children describe the movement, where to start, how to continue and where to finish. Now write the letter **s** on the board slowly and deliberately while you and the children simultaneously repeat the movement. Clean the board and invite pairs of children to the board, one to write the letter following their partner's instructions, cleaning the board in between while the children alternate their roles. Finally, ask the children to describe the movement for you to write the letter on the board. The children can practise forming the letter with their fingers in damp sand in the tray, or with a black felt pen on pupil whiteboards, or with pencil and paper.

Using your lesson plan as a guide, now discuss with the children what they have learnt today.

- **They are able to select 's' from the alphabet line.**
- **They know that the letter 's' sounds /s/.**
- **They can find it in a group of letters.**
- **They can find it at the beginning of words, in the middle of words and at the end of words.**
- **Not only can they follow the movement pattern for writing the letter 's', they can also tell someone else how to write it.**

Conclude by singing the alphabet song again.

Cleaning the board between the letter formation movements is done to avoid any risk of copying from the board, as the attention would have to be divided between the eye and the hand. The complexities of copying are described in great detail in the Montessori Method by Culverwell as long ago as 1913. He writes that, instead of relying on the eye to direct the hand, Montessori relies on the motor memory: *The fingers are trained to remember the movements needed to form the letters.* Learning this movement will help consolidate the letter in the memory, together with its visual appearance, its name and its sound.

Teaching procedure for days 2, 3, and 4

The target letter sound /a/ is taught the next day, and /t/ and /p/ on the following two days, adopting the same procedure as for the letter sound /s/. Before starting to introduce each new target letter sound, review the previous day's teaching. Resources are the same for each session except for the magnetic letters and letter and word cards for **a**, **t** and **p** (see below).

For learning 'a' sounds /a/, the cards needed are one with **a** in print, cards with **c s w a** in print and cards for the words **apple**, **sand**, **zebra**, **banana**.

For learning 't' sounds /t/, the cards needed are one with **t** in print, cards with **f r j t** in print, and cards for the words **rabbit**, **actor**, **towel**, **tent**.

For learning 'p' sounds /p/, the cards needed are one with **p** in print, cards with **g o y p** in print and cards for words **stop, Penny, pat, puppet**.

After four days of teaching, the children should be able to identify four letters of the alphabet, know their sounds, and be able to identify the letters in two contexts – in sequences of letters and in words formed from the taught letters. They should also have learnt to form the letters.

The above explicit direct teaching procedures are designed to be presented to the whole class. Practising writing the letter, after the formation procedure has been taught, can be carried out in groups.

Formative/diagnostic assessment

Ongoing formative/diagnostic assessment is an integral part of learning and teaching, and is strongly recommended in *Letters and Sounds* (DfES, 2007). At this pre-programme stage, the teacher will be able to identify from the daily sessions not only the children who are gaining alphabet knowledge and can join in with the alphabet song activity successfully, but also those children who are proceeding at a slower pace and are not confident at either singing the alphabet song and/or pointing to the letters on the magnetic alphabet simultaneously. In each of the daily sessions, the children will have been introduced to one of four basic letter sounds /s/ /a/ /t/ /p/ and the formation of their corresponding letters **s a t p**.

As the teacher displays the target letter in different positions in words, she will be able to identify those children who can pronounce the relevant sound correctly. When the children are given the target sound, the teacher can identify those children who are able to recognise the letter in different positions in words, write the related letter, or tell a partner or the teacher how to write it.

The record sheet might be as follows:

Score sheet to assess children's knowledge of the letters s a t p

Date:

Child's name	Alphabet knowledge		Can give the sound for:				Can write letters for:			
	song Yes No	with print Yes No	's'	'a'	't'	'p'	/s/	/a/	/t/	/p/

See Appendix 2 on page 116 for full photocopiable sheet.

Task 2
Having taught the letter sounds and letter formation for 3 consonants and a vowel, what do you think are the next steps to take? (Answers at the end of the chapter.)

(B) Teaching blending for word reading and segmenting for spelling

What are the children going to do with the cluster of letter sounds they have been taught? From the simple words which can be generated using these letters, how can we teach the children to read and spell them? Figure 5.3 below sets out a sequence of explicit teaching procedures for just such a purpose, namely blending for word reading and segmenting and blending for spelling. Beginner readers must be taught *how to blend (synthesise) the sounds to read words and break up (segment) the sounds in words to spell* (Rose Review (2006), para. 45).

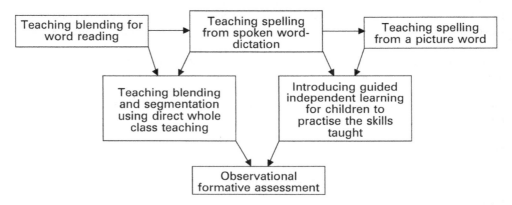

Figure 5.3 Procedures for using initial small cluster of letter sounds taught

(i) Teaching blending for word reading

The importance of the blending process in the development of independent reading is highlighted by Feitelson (1988), the skills involved bearing a causal relationship to emerging word recognition skills (Perfetti et al., 1987). The method described by Feitelson (1988) is used in Germany and Austria, which has a strong emphasis on the blending or co-articulating of letters to pronounce words. This is the synthetic phonics approach. Feitelson cites two types of blending procedure:

- **the final blending procedure of Richardson et al. (1977);**
- **the successive blending procedure of Resnick and Beck (1976).**

In Richardson's procedure, the sound of each letter is pronounced and stored in memory. The final blending procedure is only attempted after the sounds of all of the letters have been pronounced and stored in memory e.g. the word **cat.** *Point to 'c', say /k/: point to 'a', say /a/: point to 'ca', say /ka/ slowly: repeat, point to 'ca', say /ka/ quickly: point to 't', say / t/: point to 'cat', say /kat/ slowly: point to 'cat' and say /kat/ quickly and smoothly.*

In Resnick and Beck's procedure, the sounds are synthesized successively as the reader goes along e.g. *Point to the beginning of the word 'cat'. Draw your finger along underneath the word, stretching out the sound, like a piece of elastic, saying /kaaat/ then releasing the stretch, as it were, to say /kaat and /kat/: point to 'cat' and say /kat/ smoothly.*

The next step, therefore, is to teach blending for word reading. The approach advocated in *Letters and Sounds* (DfES, 2007) fits most closely with Resnick and Beck's (1976) successive blending procedure described above. We used this approach in our studies. Pupils sounded out magnetic letters from left-to-right slowly and fluently, stretching out each sound and blending it into its adjacent neighbour without a pause, to produce one single sound from the discrete successive phonemes. Liberman and Liberman (1990) call this *co-articulation*. This has the advantage of cutting out the 'uh' sound that often follows the pronunciation of letter sounds on their own. Simultaneously, the magnetic letters were pushed together from left-to-right, from the first letter through to the last letter, to form one complete word as the sounds were co-articulated. When the children do this for themselves, the use of the magnetic letters enables them to physically and visually experience the blending process. (The electronic version of our programme demonstrates the blending process by moving the letters together from left to right.)

(a) Teacher modelling the blending procedure

Target: Children will be able to demonstrate the blending procedure for word reading using magnetic letters.
Resources: Teaching magnetic board and relevant magnetic letters and arrow. Word card **pat**.

If you have a set of magnetic letters, you may find it helpful to carry out the suggested activities yourself as you read this section.

Place a magnetic arrow ▶ on the left hand side of the magnetic board as a reminder that reading is from left to right. Place the letter **a** on the magnetic board, ask the children to say the sound /a/. Leaving a space after the letter **a** place the letter **t** next to it, **a t**. Ask the children to say the sound /t/. Now demonstrate the blending process. Start to push the **a** towards the **t** while you blend the 2 sounds /a/ and /t/ together smoothly to sound /at/. Replace the magnetic letters in the alphabet line. Tell the children that when they see a word they do not know, this is the procedure to follow – sounding the letters and blending them together to read that word.

b) Children trying out the blending procedure (1)

The magnetic arrow ▶ can remain on the left hand side of the magnetic board or removed at the teacher's discretion. Place the letter **a** on the magnetic board, ask the children to say the sound /a/. Leaving a space after the letter **a** place the letter **s** next to it, **a s**. Ask the children to say the sound /s/. Then ask them to tell you what the next step is before reminding them. Start to push the **a** towards the **s** while they blend the 2 sounds /a/ and /s/ together smoothly to sound /as/ and read the word.

c) Children trying out the blending procedure (2)

Place the word **sat** on the magnetic board. Do *NOT* tell the children what this word is. Ask the children what is the first letter of the word and pull it down: **s**. The children say the sound

/s/. Similarly for the second letter of the word, pull it down alongside the first letter, leaving a space as before: **s a**. The children say the middle sound /a/. Bring down the last letter as before, alongside **s a t**, saying the sound /t/. Ask the children to say the first, middle and last sound, i.e. /s/ /a/ /t/, and then start to push the letters together from left to right, while blending the three sounds together smoothly and fluently to sound /sat/ and read **sat**.

d) Children trying out the blending procedure (3)

Display a printed word for the children to read: **pat**. Point to each letter in succession asking the children to say the sounds /p/ /a/ /t/. Then ask the children to blend the sounds together to read the word, smoothly co-articulating the letter sounds. The children read the word **pat**.

(In teaching observations we sometimes see the teachers doing the sounding and blending, with the children listening, but it is most important that the children do this themselves.)

ii) Teaching segmenting for spelling

What do children have to do to spell a word? Children have to:

- **be able to break down the spoken word into its letter sounds (phonemes);**
- **remember the order of the letter sounds;**
- **remember the letter shape (the grapheme) for each sound;**
- **blend the letter sounds together to check that the phonemes in the spoken word map on to the sequence of letters in the printed word.**

a) Procedure for teaching segmenting for word spelling

Target:	Children will demonstrate the segmenting procedure for spelling a dictated word.
Resources:	Teaching magnetic board, relevant magnetic letters and direction arrow as before.

This time the children do not see the target word, they hear it. Say that you want them to help you to spell the word **sat** as in 'The puppy **sat** on the mat. Spell the word **sat**'.

Ask the children to:

- **repeat the word for spelling** *sat;*
- **say the first sound in** *sat* **(i.e. /s/);**
- **find the letter for the sound from the magnetic alphabet and place it on the board s;**
- **say the second sound in** *sat* **(i.e. /a/);**
- **find the letter from the alphabet and place it next to the first letter on the board s a;**
- **say the last sound in** *sat* **(i.e. /t/), find the letter from the alphabet and place it next to the first two letters on the board s a t.**

Now ask the children to say each sound /s/ /a/ /t/ and blend the sounds together, as for word reading, to make **sat**. Replace the magnetic letters on the alphabet line. Blending the letter sounds together is carried out to check that the sounds in the spoken word map on to the sequence of letters in the printed word.

REFLECTIVE TASK

REFLECTIVE TASK

Task 3

How many words can you make from the letters **s a t p**. (Answers at end of chapter.)

b) Introducing guided independent learning with pupil magnetic boards – skills application

We now want the children to apply the skills they have acquired by working independently, each with a pupil magnetic board or in pairs, sharing a pupil magnetic board and relevant magnetic letters. The pupil magnetic boards are fitted with an alphabet grid and as each letter sound is taught the relevant magnetic letter is placed on the boards. The display below illustrates that at this stage the magnetic letters on the board are **a p s t** together with a magnetic arrow to signify the left-hand side where the children will start to spell the word. The letters not in bold represent the letters which will only be placed on the alphabet grid after they have been taught.

```
a b c d e f g h i j k l m
n o p q r s t u v w x y z

→
```

(i) Dictated words

Children are asked to spell a word on their magnetic boards. The teacher dictates 'Spell **past**. My birthday is **past**. Spell the word **past**.'

After checking how the children have carried out the task and asking them to read the word produced, namely '**past**', the teacher spells the word on the teaching magnetic board, inviting children to carry out the procedures and replace the letters in the alphabet line as before.

Children replace the letters used on their pupil magnetic boards to their alphabetic position on the grid ready to use again.

(ii) Picture words

Instead of a dictated word, children are given/shown a picture, e.g. a **tap**, and are asked to say the word themselves and spell it on their boards using the same procedures as for dictated words.

(C) Formative/diagnostic assessment

This is ongoing during each session both through observation of how the children carry out the blending and segmenting procedures during explicit direct teaching, and also through checking how the children carry out each of the tasks given for the guided independent learning.

The heading for a record sheet might be as follows below. A code is devised for the recording of blending competence, for example:

1 = unable to blend;
2 = cannot produce the correct sound for any letter;
3 = can produce the correct sound for one of the letters;
4 = can produce the correct sound for all of the letters;
5 = can sound and blend successfully.

The word reading and segmentation for spelling takes place after the basic teaching of the three consonants and one vowel has been completed. Knowledge of the alphabet can be included again in this record sheet as some of the children who were working at a slower pace earlier on may have made some progress by now.

Score sheet to assess children's ability to sound and blend the letters s a t p

									Alphabet				Segmentation		
Child's name	Blending				Blending				Song		Print		Dictation		Picture
	as	at	sap	sat	tap	taps	pat	pats	Y	N	Y	N	pats	taps	tap

See Appendix 3 on page 117 for full photocopiable sheet.

REFLECTIVE TASK

Task 4
Recording segmenting for spelling using s a t p
What sort of spelling record of children's progress would you as a teacher find it useful to make before proceeding with the full programme? Devise a record-keeping code for segmentation for spelling from dictation and from a picture (suggestions for content at end of chapter).

(D) Overview of basic skills acquisition procedures

The following figure illustrates an overview of the basic procedures adopted for children starting to blend phonemes with graphemes to read words, starting to segment words into sounds and starting to form letters to spell words.

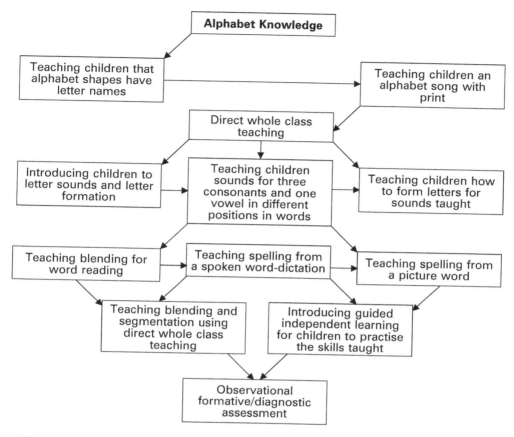

Figure 5.4 Overview of the basic procedures required in the synthetic phonics programme

The teacher's role in implementing the above procedures would be:

- selecting the target(s) to be reached;
- selecting and preparing the relevant resources;
- setting the scene (alphabet song activity with magnetic alphabet and letters);
- modelling the target skill(s) for the children to try out – skills acquisition;
- providing for guided independent practice and learning – skills application;
- evaluating learning through observational formative/diagnostic assessment.

A SUMMARY OF **KEY POINTS**

> Children need to learn that letters must be connected to their sounds in order to pronounce unfamiliar printed words.

> To help children acquire alphabet knowledge, they are taught an alphabet song with print using lower and upper case magnetic letters as they share the same letter names and letter sounds.

> Using direct whole class teaching, children are taught a small cluster of sounds in different positions in words together with letter formation. They should be able to identify these letters in sequences of letters and in words formed from the taught letters.

> Blending for word reading and segmenting for spelling are explicitly taught using whole class direct teaching, magnetic boards and letters. The children also practise spelling from dictation and from picture words through guided independent learning.
> Formative assessment is ongoing through observation of pupil response during explicit direct teaching and monitoring tasks carried out during guided independent learning.
> A diagrammatic overview (see page 59) describes the basic procedures required in the synthetic phonics programme together with the teacher's role in implementing these procedures.

Reflective task answers

Task 1

The children can learn:

- that an alphabet has shapes, shapes are letters and letters have names;
- the alphabetic order of the letter names;
- that lower and upper case letters share the same letter name;
- to follow a left-to-right direction of print;
- to start at the beginning;
- to finish at the end.

Task 2

The next steps would be:

- teaching blending for word reading;
- teaching segmenting for spelling.

Task 3

Words: a, as, at, pat, Pat, pats, sap, sat, tap, taps, past, Papa.

Task 4
Recording segmenting for spelling using s a t p

A segmentation code could take account of what children have to do to spell a word and the columns could be Yes Nearly No

1 = Can the pupil break down the spoken word into its letter sounds (phonemes)?
2 = Can the pupil remember the order of the letter sounds (phonemes) in the word?
3 = Can the pupil remember the letter shape (grapheme) for each sound?
4 = Can the pupil blend the letter sounds together to check that the sounds (phonemes) in the spoken word map on to the sequence of letters in the printed word?

REFERENCES REFERENCES **REFERENCES** REFERENCES **REFERENCES** REFERENCES
Culverwell, E. P. (1913) *The Montessori Principles and Practice.* London: Bell & Sons.
Department for Education and Skills (DfES) (2007). *Letters and Sounds.* London: DfES.
    www.standards.dfes.gov.uk/local/clld/las.html

Feitelson, D. (1988) *Facts and Fads in Beginning Reading. A Cross-Language Perspective.* Norwood NJ: Ablex.

Liberman I. Y. and Liberman A. M. (1990). Whole language vs. Code Emphasis. Underlying Assumptions and Their Implications for Reading Instruction. *Bulletin of the Orton Society,* Vol.XXXX, Orton Dyslexia Society.

Perfetti C. A., Beck I., Bell, L. and Hughes C. (1987). Phonemic knowledge and learning to read are reciprocal: A longitudinal study of first grade children. *Merrill-Palmer Quarterly,* 33: 283–319.

Resnick L. B. and Beck I. L. (1976). Designing instruction in reading: Interaction of theory and practice, in J. T. Guthrie (Ed.) *Aspects of Reading Acquisition.* Baltimore, MD: Johns Hopkins University Press.

Richardson E., Di Benedetto, B. and Bradley C. M. (1977) The relationship of sound blending to reading achievement. *Review of Educational Research,* 47: 319–34.

Rose Review (2006) *Independent Review of the Teaching of Early Reading: Final Report.* Nottingham: DfES.

Watson, J. E. (1998) An investigation of the effects of phonics teaching on children's progress in reading and spelling. PhD thesis. University of St Andrews.

Watson, J. E. and Johnston, R. S. (2007) *Fast Phonics First* (part of Rigby Star Phonics). Oxford: Harcourt.

Watson J. E. and Johnston R. S. (2000) *Accelerating Reading and Spelling with Synthetic Phonics: a guide to the teaching method.* Scottish Executive Education Department. Available from Learning and Teaching Scotland, The Optima, 58 Robertson Street, Glasgow G2 8DU.

6
Teaching a synthetic phonics lesson in Phase 2 of *Letters and Sounds*

Learning objectives

In this chapter you will learn how to:

- follow a sample lesson format for teaching a Phase 2 synthetic phonics lesson;
- share targets and success criteria with your children;
- plan quickfire revision of previously taught sounds, and of words used for reading and spelling the day before;
- teach the new letter sound and how to use it for word reading, spelling and letter formation;
- dictate words for spelling using a word-sentence-word procedure;
- introduce irregular words, captions and sentences for reading and spelling;
- evaluate your children's learning regularly for formative/diagnostic assessment purposes;
- analyse decodable readers for fit with progress in letter sound learning, to maximise learning potential.

Those recommended for the award of Qualified Teacher Status (QTS) should meet the following Professional Standards:

Q12: Know a range of approaches to assessment, including the importance of formative assessment.

Q22: Plan for progression across the age and ability range for which they are trained, designing effective learning sequences within lessons and across series of lessons and demonstrating secure subject/curriculum knowledge.

Q25: Teach lessons and sequences of lessons across the age and ability range for which they are trained in which they:

(a) use a range of strategies and resources including e-learning taking practical account of diversity and promoting equality and inclusion;

(b) build on prior knowledge, develop concepts and processes, enable learners to apply new knowledge, understanding and skills and meet learning objectives;

(c) adapt their language to suit the learners they teach, introducing new ideas and concepts clearly and using explanations, questions, discussions and plenaries effectively;

(d) demonstrate the ability to manage the learning of individuals, groups and whole classes, modifying their teaching to suit the stage of the lesson.

Q26:

(a) Make effective use of a range of assessment, monitoring and recording strategies;

(b) Assess the learning needs of those they teach in order to set challenging learning objectives;

Q27: Provide timely, accurate and constructive feedback on learners' attainment, progress and areas of development.

Q28: Support and guide learners to reflect on their learning, identify the progress they have made and identify their emerging learning needs.

Q29: Evaluate the impact of their teaching on the progress of all learners and modify their planning and classroom practice where necessary.

Introduction

Teaching a synthetic phonics lesson

In this chapter, we will explain how to integrate all the basic elements described in Chapter 5 into one sample lesson format. We will provide an example of this lesson format showing how to teach the letter sound /d/, and how to blend for reading and segment for spelling using this and previously taught letters for reading and spelling. In Chapter 7 we will show how to teach the vowel digraph sound /oy/ and how to blend and segment letters and syllables for reading and spelling using the same lesson format. Both sample lessons follow the order of letter sound teaching recommended in *Letters and Sounds* (DfES, 2007) for the Foundation Stage (Primary 1 in Scotland) and Key Stage 1 (Primary 2 and 3 in Scotland). The single consonant 'd' from Phase 2, and the vowel digraph 'oy' from Phase 5, have been chosen to demonstrate that the programme can be *followed consistently and carefully, each day, reinforcing and building on previous learning to secure children's progress* (Rose Review, 2006, para 56).

Chapter overview

(A) Lesson format

(i)   Introduction
(ii)   Revision
(iii)   Teaching – skills acquisition
(iv)   Practice
(v)   Apply skills acquired
(vi)   Learning outcomes
(vii)   Formative assessment
(viii) Summary of teaching sequence

(B) Variations in lesson format, and integration with text reading

(i)   Some possible variations to the lesson plan
(ii)   Decodable books and graded readers

(A) Lesson format

Having taught the basic procedures adopted throughout the programme (see Chapter 5), the children are now ready to start doing synthetic phonics lessons. Figure 6.1 following shows the teaching sequence which is used to deliver the programme for:

- whole class explicit direct teaching – skills acquisition;
- children in groups at their tables – practising the skills acquired;
- children in groups at their tables – application of skills acquired.

Opportunities for skills development outside the lesson format will be described separately (see pages 000).

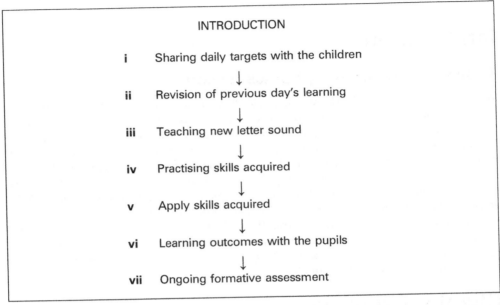

INTRODUCTION

i Sharing daily targets with the children

↓

ii Revision of previous day's learning

↓

iii Teaching new letter sound

↓

iv Practising skills acquired

↓

v Apply skills acquired

↓

vi Learning outcomes with the pupils

↓

vii Ongoing formative assessment

Figure 6.1. Lesson format – sequence for teaching a synthetic phonics lesson

(i) Introduction to lesson to teach letter sound /d/

We are going to show a sample lesson based on the procedures outlined in *Letters and Sounds* (DfES, 2007), but fleshed out with our own experience of implementing a successful synthetic phonics programme. In our programme *Fast Phonics First* (Watson and Johnston, 2007), which is based on the programme we used in Clackmannanshire:

- the alphabet song (with print) which signifies for the children the start of the session and continues to help children consolidate their alphabet knowledge;
- targets for the session are shared with the children, talking through what they already know and what they are now going to learn;
- the daily lesson plan to provide a structured guide for sharing the target outcomes for the day. The children need to know the expected success criteria. Table 6.2 below shows a structured format you can use to prompt you for the sequence of activities in the lesson. It can also be used for making notes during the Learning Outcomes plenary session.

Table 6.1 Structured guide for target sharing

Focus of discussion	Criteria for success	Learning outcomes
Revision **m**	Say the letter and the sound Read four words Spell four words	
Lesson new letter **d**	Say the letter and the sound Find the letter in words, say beginning middle end	
Words with **d**	Read four words Spell four words Write **d**	
Magnetic boards	d added to alphabet grid Spell word from teacher Spell two picture words	
a is both a letter and a word Captions	Read captions Spell captions with teacher	

For the children, at this early stage in the programme, a brief outline to which they can refer can be displayed in a prominent place for reference. It might look something like Table 6.2 below. The second column is meant for the pupils; we have put in the first column to explain it to you.

Table 6.2 Today's lesson

alphabet song	♫ ♫
revision	↻ **m**
lesson	☎ 'd' /d/
find	◎ ■.._ _.■._ _ _ _.■
reading words spelling words writing letter	**blend and read** **segment and spell** ✎ **d**
spell with magnetic letters	a b c d e f g h i j k l m n o p q r s t u v w x y z ✍
'tricky' words, captions and sentences	**read and spell**
learning outcomes	☺ ☹
alphabet song	♫ ♫

It is economical to design a chart that would only need the revision letter and the new letter changed each day, remembering to change the target letter each day to **bold** print in the box with the alphabet letters replicating the pupils' magnetic board. The symbol ↻ signifies returning to the lesson for the day before. The sound of the target letter is represented by the 📞 symbol, while the symbol that looks like two eyes 👀 indicates visually searching for the letter in the words. The dashes - - - - represent the letters in a word, and dashes with the bullet point (- - - - ▪) show where the letter **d** is situated. The pupils have to find **d** and say whether it is at the beginning, middle or end of the word. The symbol 👥 has been used to indicate children working in pairs on the magnetic boards. The happy and sad symbols ☺ ☹ indicate the Learning Outcomes section, where the children assess how well they have learnt the lesson. While it is hoped most of the children will feel they have been successful, some of them may want more help.

REFLECTIVE TASK

Task 1
Design your own chart suitable for use by your pupils so that they know how the day's lesson will proceed.

(ii) Revision

Quickfire revision.

- The most recent letter sound correspondences taught before *d*, namely *i n m*. Display letter cards one at a time, children pronounce the relevant sound and vice versa, adult pronounces each sound, children find the correct letter cards.
- Sound-talk for the children to practise oral blending and segmentation, e.g.

    D-a-d is s-a-d.   P-a-m sat on the m-a-t.   Can you s-i-t on a chair?

    Suggested words for children to practise sound-talk themselves: pin, doll, train.
- Word reading – display the previous day's spelling words, e.g. 'Tim', 'man', 'mat', 'map', and ask the children to read them (if they can), or sound, blend and read them.
- Spelling words – pronounce each of the previous day's reading words, e.g. 'Sam' 'am' 'mats' 'Pam' and ask the children to spell them by telling you how to write each letter. (Not only is this quicker than actually asking the children to come out and select magnetic letters or write the letters to spell the words, but also the purpose of telling the teacher how to write them is to see if the children can remember the procedural movement.)

(iii) Teaching the new letter sound, using it for word reading, spelling and letter formation

As described in Chapter 5, introduce the new letter sound in magnetic and print forms. Using direct whole class teaching, and the teacher's magnetic board and letters:

- Introduce the new letter sound *'d' (letter name) sounds /d/*, modelled by the teacher, with the children repeating 'd' sounds /d/.
- Find the position in words (remember – a visual search, not reading!). Display the words *stand damp add Adam*. Ask children to find the letter for /d/ in each word and circle the letter, saying whether it is at the beginning, middle or end of each word. Alternatively, if following *Letters and Sounds* (DfES, 2007), use letter fans.

- Reading words – *and dip did dim*. Children *see* the magnetic word/printed word, e.g. *dip*, but it is not pronounced for them. The children sound each letter /d/ /i/ /p/ in turn, then they blend the separate sounds together while the teacher or a child pushes the magnetic letters together to form the word. When the word is in print, the children draw their fingers along the word as they blend the sounds together. (Our electronic programme, *Fast Phonics First* (Watson and Johnston, 2007), carries out the blending process on the electronic whiteboard by pushing the letters together to form the word both automatically and manually.) Repeat the procedure for the other words.
- Spelling words – *pad Dan*. Reversing the reading procedure, the children *hear* the word /pad/, they segment it into individual sounds /p/ /a/ /d/, and a corresponding letter is selected from the teacher's magnetic alphabet as each phoneme is segmented. Each letter is placed on the teaching magnetic board with a space between the letters as in *p a d*. Children then blend the sounds and the letters are pushed together by the teacher or a child as they say the word /pad/. The magnetic letters are replaced into their position on the teacher's magnetic alphabet. Repeat the procedure for the word /Dan/. (This provides an opportunity to use the upper case version of the letter.)
- Letter formation – as in Chapter 5, teach the formation of the letter 'd', talking through the description of the procedural movement while writing the letter to support the children's cognitive processes and motor memory.

(iv) Practising skills acquired

Children are now in groups at their tables and are going to use their magnetic boards and letters. The display below reproduces the pupil magnetic boards with the alphabet grid. At this stage the magnetic letters on the board are **ad i m n p s t**, together with a magnetic arrow to signify the left-hand side where the children will start to spell the word. Ask children to add the letter for today's sound /d/.

The children are now going to use their magnetic boards and letters to spell words from dictation and from pictures. They can share the pupil magnetic boards and work in pairs, thus introducing the 'peer interaction element' of co-operative learning (Lyman, 1981). Presenting each word for spelling in the context of a sentence demonstrates how words have meaning.

- *Dictated word* – children are asked to 'spell the word *dim*. The light went *dim*. Spell the word *dim*'. After checking how the children have carried out the task and asking them to read the word, you spell and write it again for reinforcement on your board, with the children telling you the movement for each letter. The children can confirm that the spelling on their magnetic board is the same as on your board, then replace the letters on their alphabet grid ready for use again.
- *Picture words* – two pictures are normally given for each lesson. Give the children pictures of a *sad* face. You may need to discuss what kind of face it is to elicit from the children the word *sad*. Ask the children to say the word and spell it, using the same procedure as before. You then must spell and write the word on the board from the children's descriptions of the movements, as before, so that they can check their spelling with the spelling on the board, and then replace their letters on the alphabet grid.

- The second picture for *d* is of a helicopter *pad*. To elicit the word *pad*, discuss with the children that a helicopter can land on this, a *pad*. The children then follow the same procedure as that described above to say and spell the word on their magnetic boards. You will then spell and write the word on the board from their descriptions as before so that the children can check their own spelling. They can then replace the letters on their alphabet grids ready for use again.

Gradually, the children will be able to change from magnetic boards and letters to pencil and paper spelling, which will provide an opportunity to practise letter writing.

(v) Applying skills acquired

This segment of the lesson combines the teaching of irregular words and using them in captions and sentences together with words containing taught letters and the new letter. (With our programme, *Fast Phonics First* (Watson and Johnston, 2007), these are treated as separate language sessions carried out after a set of letter sounds has been taught).

(a) Irregular words

These are introduced on the basis of when their constituent letters have been taught and on their degree of frequency in the English language. You might teach irregular words other than those outlined in *Letters and Sounds* (DfES, 2007) if they are needed for reading books. For example, you can teach 'said' by the time you teach the letter **d**, as all the other letter sounds will have been taught by this stage.

Irregular words are not taught as sight words. They are taught by encouraging children to examine the words to identify known letter sounds, and to search for similarities and differences with known words before the teacher helps them to read the words. Applying and developing the skills they are acquiring enables pupils to participate in and actively interact with text.

(b) Reading and spelling captions and sentences

The children have previously been introduced to **a** as a letter, so it is now explained to them that **a** can also be a word. Using the letters which have been introduced up to and including the example **d**, children can be asked to read captions, e.g. 'a tin' and 'a sad man'. Captions can be dictated for children to spell with magnetic letters, e.g. 'a tin pan', and to say and spell the caption from a picture of 'a tin'.

(vi) Learning outcomes

You can use Table 6.1 as a guide for this plenary session (see page 65). There is a column for your notes as you discuss the success criteria with the children. From your own observations you will know what the children have achieved. You now want to know *how successful the children thought they were* as you go through the expected success criteria with them and whether any specific part is causing problems. Notes you have made on the children's learning can be taken into account in the formative assessment element of the programme.

Conclude the session by singing the alphabet song with print again.

(vii) Ongoing formative/diagnostic assessment

Formative assessment is ongoing throughout the delivery of the programme through:

- discussions with the pupils about what they have learnt during the session;
- observation of how the children carry out the blending and segmenting procedures during explicit direct teaching;
- monitoring how the children carry out each of the tasks given in the practice sessions;
- checking how children apply the skills being acquired.

It would be useful for a record sheet to be completed after a set of letter sounds has been taught. In this way, you can identify which children might be needing extra support during the programme, whether some extra time might need to be taken to consolidate what has been taught before proceeding to the next lesson, and whether teaching might need to be adapted to take account of formative assessment findings (Rose Review, 2006).

(viii) Summary of the above sequence

The following figure illustrates the teaching sequence described above.

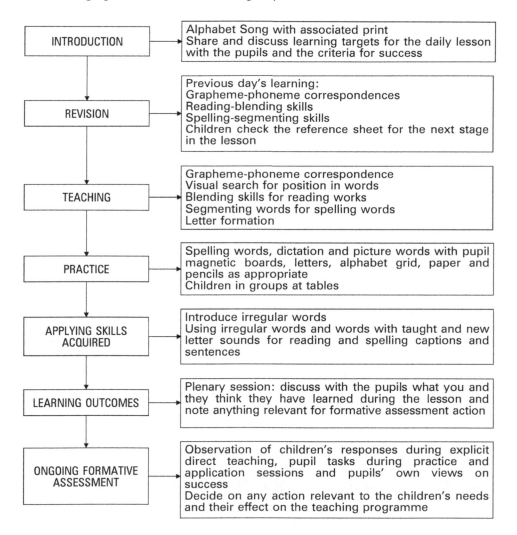

Figure 6.2 Summary of a typical teaching sequence in the programme

(B) Variations in lesson format, and integration with text reading

(i) Some possible variations to the lesson plan

(a) Language sessions

The consonant **d** that was used as the example for describing how to teach a lesson was taken from Phase 2 of *Letters and Sounds* (DfES, 2007). An order for teaching the Phase 2 letters in *Letters and Sounds* (DfES, 2007) is given in Table 6.3 below, at the rate of one set of four letters per week.

Table 6.3 Phase 2: Graphemes and irregular and high-frequency words

Phase 2	Sets of graphemes (to be taught in the context of words)					Irregular/high-frequency words
2. 1	s	a	t	p		
2 .2	i	n	m .	d		is, it, in, at
2. 3	g	o	c	k		and
2. 4	ck	e	u	r		to, the
2. 5	h	b	f, ff	l, ll	ss	I, no, go

Using a day to teach each grapheme or letter sound, it is possible to teach blocks of four to five letter sounds, and then to take a day for consolidation, and to work on irregular word and caption reading. This is what we did in our programme in Clackmannanshire. For our studies, we had separate language sessions where we combined learning how to read and spelling irregular words with using them in captions and sentences (using previously taught letters).

(b) Guided Independent Learning

In our studies, we also included a Guided Independent Learning task, to be presented as the final part of each session for consolidation (but it could be done later in the day). When teaching **d**, our procedure was as follows:

- on an alphabet line, the children were asked to point to the letter for /d/, the teacher indicated *d* on the alphabet, and the children said the sound;
- the words 'stand' 'damp' 'add' and 'Adam' were presented to the children on sheets of paper, for a visual search – they were asked to point to or circle the letter for /d/, saying whether it was at the beginning, middle or end of the word;
- the children practised writing the letter 'd' with pencil and paper.

Such activities will help you assess the children's learning. You can see if they can find the letter sound when it is spoken and see if they can detect the letter in printed words. You can also monitor how their letter formation skills are progressing.

(ii) Decodable books and graded readers

It is imperative that the phonics sessions are not perceived to be a separate entity in their own right. These phonic sessions should not be divorced from text reading, which is the practical activity where the children can apply and develop the skills they have been learning during the delivery of the phonics programme. A series of decodable readers matched to each set of taught letter sounds can be used, where the children get practice in reading captions and sentences using regular and irregular words made up of the taught letter sounds. Grammatically such readers are likely to be progressive, providing experience for the children of reading:

- captions;
- one sentence to a page, then two sentences to a page;
- one syllable, and then two syllable compound words;
- nouns, proper nouns, plurals;
- pronouns, personal pronouns;
- verbs, present and past tense;
- adjectives, adverbs;
- speech bubbles leading to direct speech;
- commas, prepositions, conjunctions, questions, exclamation marks.

If such decodable readers are not available, a series of graded readers at the relevant level can be used, starting after the letters of Set 4 (see Table 6.3) have been taught. If you do this, you will need to teach any additional irregular words found in the books.

The 'real' reading situation provides a further opportunity for formative assessment. The teacher can identify which child(ren) might be needing extra support, and a short-term needs group can be formed to revisit the specific aspect of the programme causing a problem.

REFLECTIVE TASK

Task 2

Try to write some linked captions and sentences for a first decodable reader using only the letters from s, a, t, p, i, n, m, and d, two vowels and six consonants. Indicate any art work you think might be appropriate. Analyse the text for what you think the children will have learnt. (Example at the end of the chapter.)

A SUMMARY OF **KEY POINTS**

> This chapter explained how to integrate all the basic elements described in Chapter 5 into one sample lesson format, starting with sharing the target outcomes for the day with your pupils. It is important that they know the criteria for success.

> The revision aspect of the lesson format is described in detail, followed by the teaching of the new letter sound for word reading, spelling and letter formation, using whole class direct teaching.

> To practise and apply the skills acquired, the children now work in pairs with pupil magnetic boards and letters, thus setting the scene for co-operative learning. As well as spelling dictated and picture words, irregular words are introduced together with reading captions and sentences.

> The Learning Outcomes aspect of the lesson relates to the sharing of the day's targets. From your own observations using formative assessment, you will know what the children have achieved and whether there are individual needs to be addressed. What is important now is how successful the children think they have been.

> A summary of the aforementioned teaching sequence in the programme is displayed in diagrammatic form (see page 69).
> The importance of including decodable or graded readers is also discussed in some detail to integrate the phonic sessions and 'real reading'.

Reflective task answers
Task 2

Words from two sets of letter s, a, t, p, i, n, m, d

s	a	t	p	i	n	m	d
sap	a	tap	Pat pat	in	Nan	map	dim
sat	an	tin	pan	is	Nip nip	mat	din
sip	as	tip	pin	it	nap	man	dip
sit	at	Tim	Pip pip	imp	Nana	mats	Dan
Sid	am	taps	pit		nips	maps	Dad
sits	Ann	tips	Pam				dims
sips	add	tins	pad				dips
	and		pads				
	ant		pans				
	ants		pins				
	Anna		pips				
			pats				
			Papa				

Below are examples of linked captions and sentences using words from the above table. Please note that no irregular words will have been introduced yet but reference is made here to relevant high frequency words, namely 'is', 'it', 'in', 'at'. Suggested appropriate artwork and grammatical features are included.

Caption/Sentence	Artwork	Learning potential
Tim and Anna	Boy and girl playing in the garden with a 'Wendy' house.	Capital letters for names. Introducing conjunction 'and'.
Tim, Anna and Pip	Pip, a playful kitten added to the above scene.	Introducing a comma between Tim and Anna.
Tim taps a tin	Same scene but with Tim tapping a tin with a drum stick. Another empty tin lies beside him.	Introducing a sentence, starts with a capital letter and ends with a full stop: 'taps' as a verb, 'a' as a word and an adjective.

Anna taps a pan	Same scene but with Anna tapping a pan with a drum stick. Another empty pan lies beside her.	As above.
Pip sits in a pan	Same scene as above but with Pip sitting in what was the empty pan.	As above. Introducing preposition 'in'.
Pip sits in a tin	Same scene as above but with Pip sitting in what was the empty tin. The pan is lying upside down as Pip tipped it over.	As above.
Tim taps Pip's tin	Same scene as above. Tim has left his tin and comes over to Pip's tin to tap it with his drumstick. Pip scampers out of the tin.	As above. Introducing the use of an apostrophe.
Anna and Tim pat Pip	Scene now with two tins and two pans and two drum sticks lying about. Pip sitting beside Anna and Tim who are stroking and patting the kitten.	Concluding sentence. A title for the linked captions and sentences might be 'Tim, Anna and Pip'.

REFERENCES REFERENCES **REFERENCES** REFERENCES **REFERENCES** REFERENCES

DfES (2007) *Letters and Sounds*. London: DfES. **www.standards.dfes.gov.uk/local/clld/las.html**

Lyman, F. (1981) *Think, Pair, Share.* **www.eazhull.org.uk/nlc/think,_pair,_share.htm**

Rose Review (2006) *Independent Review of the Teaching of Early Reading: Final Report.* Nottingham: DfES.

Watson, J. E. and Johnston, R. S. (2007) *Fast Phonics First* (part of Rigby Star Phonics). Oxford: Harcourt.

7
Teaching Phases 3 to 6 of
Letters and Sounds

Learning objectives

In this chapter you will learn how to:

- **teach a Phase 5 synthetic phonics lesson;**
- **identify consonant digraphs, vowel digraphs and adjacent consonants;**
- **divide words visually into syllables for reading;**
- **teach syllable blending for word reading;**
- **segment words into syllables and then phonemes for spelling;**
- **add prefix and suffix morphemes to root words;**
- **dictate sentences including the taught graphemes, and irregular and high-frequency words;**
- **assess the children's learning against stated criteria for success;**
- **use the detailed daily lesson plans as forward planning for the weekly plan, which in turn fits in with the long-term curriculum plan.**

Those recommended for the award of Qualified Teacher Status (QTS) should meet the following Professional Standards.

Q12: Know a range of approaches to assessment, including the importance of formative assessment.

Q22: Plan for progression across the age and ability range for which they are trained, designing effective learning sequences within lessons and across series of lessons and demonstrating secure subject/curriculum knowledge.

Q25: Teach lessons and sequences of lessons across the age and ability range for which they are trained in which they:

> (a) use a range of strategies and resources including e-learning taking practical account of diversity and promoting equality and inclusion;

> (b) build on prior knowledge, develop concepts and processes, enable learners to apply new knowledge, understanding and skills and meet learning objectives;

> (c) adapt their language to suit the learners they teach, introducing new ideas and concepts clearly and using explanations, questions, discussions and plenaries effectively;

> (d) demonstrate the ability to manage the learning of individuals, groups and whole classes, modifying their teaching to suit the stage of the lesson.

Q26:

> (a) Make effective use of a range of assessment, monitoring and recording strategies;

> (b) Assess the learning needs of those they teach in order to set challenging learning objectives.

Q27: Provide timely, accurate and constructive feedback on learners' attainment, progress and areas of development.

Introduction

Chapter overview

In this chapter, we will explain the phonic progression in *Letters and Sounds* (DfES, 2007) in Phases 3 to 6, and show you how the Phase 2 lesson plan in Chapter 6 can also be used for the subsequent phases of the phonics programme. In order to do this we will give a fully worked out example of a Phase 5 lesson, showing you how to teach the vowel digraph **oy**.

This chapter is divided into the following sections.

(A) Phases 3 and 4 of *Letters and Sounds*: beyond single letter-sound correspondences.
(B) Phase 5: spelling alternatives (and a sample lesson), alternative pronunciations, and syllabification.
(C) Phase 6: introducing morphemes.
(D) Pace of delivery of programme.
(E) Curriculum implications.

(A) Phases 3 and 4 of *Letters and Sounds*: beyond single letter-sound correspondences

(i) Phase 3: less frequent letter sounds and the introduction of consonant and vowel digraphs

In Chapter 6, we showed you the *Letters and Sounds* order for teaching consonants and vowels in Phase 2 of the programme. For your convenience, this is repeated below in Table 7.1, together with the relevant irregular and high-frequency words. Each line represents one week's teaching.

Table 7.1: Phase 2 Graphemes and irregular and high-frequency words

Phase 2	Sets of graphemes (to be taught also in the context of words)				Irregular/high-frequency words
2.1	s	a	t	p	
2.2	i	n	m	d	is, it, in, at
2.3	g	o	c	k	and
2.4	ck	e	u	r	to, the
2.5	h	b	f,ff	l,ll, ss	no, go, I
2.6	Revise all graphemes and sounds taught so far				

You will note that although **ck, ff, ll** and **ss** consist of two graphemes, the phoneme correspondence is /k/, /f/, /l/, and /s/. *Letters and Sounds* suggests that Phase 2 should take about six weeks to teach, allowing a week for revision and consolidation.

When compiling such a sequence, the authors of *Letters and Sounds* will have been aware of the need to separate letters of graphic similarity, as they might confuse some children. It might be useful for you to know that there are clearly defined *groups of letters with graphic similarity* (Dunn-Rankin, 1968), such as:

- e, a, s, c, o
- f, l, t, k, i, h
- b, d, p, o, g, h
- n, u, m, w, h

The letters **j, q, v, x** and **z** were excluded in Dunn-Rankin's research because of their infrequent use in primary readers. *Letters and Sounds* introduces these five letters (together with **w** and **y**) quite late on, as the first two sets of letters for Phase 3.

Up to this point, the children will have learnt that one letter stands for one sound. However, in English, there are more speech sounds than there are letters of the alphabet. Morris (1990) illustrates this as follows:

ENGLISH WORDS

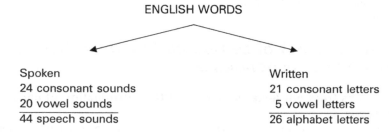

Spoken	Written
24 consonant sounds	21 consonant letters
20 vowel sounds	5 vowel letters
44 speech sounds	26 alphabet letters

This means that some sounds are connected to more than one letter, e.g. the letters **c** and **h** as in /church/, and **s** and **h** as in /shop/, come together to sound /ch/ and /sh/ respectively. These are known as consonant digraphs. Similarly, the letters **a** and **i** come together to form a vowel digraph for the long vowel /ā/ as in /pail/, see also **oi** as in /coin/. It is common practice to teach phonics in this order: the simple consonant and vowel correspondences, then the more complex consonant and vowel digraphs. These digraphs are introduced in Phase 3 when all the single letter sounds have been taught. The progression for Phase 3 is shown in Table 7.2; each line represents one week's teaching.

Letters and Sounds (DfES, 2007) suggests that Phases 2 and 3 together should take about 18 weeks maximum to complete, which allows time for practice and consolidation.

(ii) Phase 4: adjacent consonants

In Chapter 4, we showed that Phase 4 covers adjacent consonants (or consonant blends), that is, a sequence of consonants at the beginning or end of words, e.g. clap, string, post. The purpose of Phase 4 is described by *Letters and Sounds* (DfES, 2007) as being *to consolidate children's knowledge of graphemes in reading and spelling words containing adjacent consonants*. A bank of suggested words is provided from which you can select those needed for an activity. In Table 7.3 we have selected one word for each day as an

Table 7.2: Phase 3 Graphemes, consonant digraphs, vowel digraphs, and irregular and high-frequency words

Phase 3	Sets of graphemes (to be taught also in the context of words)				Irregular/high-frequency words
3.1	j	v	w	x	Revise preceding words
3.2	y	z, zz	qu		he, she
	Consonant digraphs, vowel digraphs				
3.3	ch	sh	th **th**	ng	we, me, be
3.4	ai	ee	igh	oa	was
3.5	oo **oo**	ar	or	ur	my
3.6	ow (cow)	oi	ear	air	you
3.7	ure	er			they
3.8	**Consolidation** Teach: reading and spelling of irregular/ high-frequency words. Practise: all GPCs*; letter names; blending for reading; segmentation for spelling; two-syllable words; reading and writing captions and sentences.				her
3.9					all
3.10					are
3.11	More consolidation if necessary or move to Phase 4.				

*Grapheme to phoneme correspondences

example, but bear in mind that Annex B of *The Primary Framework for Literacy and Mathematics* (Primary National Strategy, 2006) says that you should not teach lists of similar words such as 'best', 'nest', 'vest', in one lesson. One line represents one week's teaching.

Table 7.3: Phase 4 Adjacent consonants

Phase 4	Adjacent consonants				Irregular and high-frequency words
4.1	desk	wasp	best	shift	said, so, he, she, we
4.2	skip	spot	step	spoil	have, like, some, come
4.3	**Consolidation** Teach: reading and spelling of irregular/ high-frequency words. Practise: Phase 2/3 graphemes; reading adjacent consonant words; spelling adjacent consonant words; reading and writing sentences				were, there, little, one, all, are
4.4					do, when, out, what

You will see again that a few weeks are available for consolidation, but the teaching of irregular and high-frequency words has been speeded up from Phase 3. Phases 2 to 4 together are expected to take a maximum of 24 weeks teaching, to be completed before the end of Reception (Primary 1).

REFLECTIVE TASK

Task 1

Try to complete the table below with words that fit into the categories of initial adjacent consonants (ccvc) words, final adjacent consonants (cvcc) words, initial and final adjacent consonants (ccvcc) words, and in initial and final adjacent consonants (cccvcc and ccvccc) words.

ccvc words	cvcc words	ccvcc words	cccvcc words	ccvccc
frog	lamp	chest	thrust	brunch

(B) Phase 5

In *Letters and Sounds* (DfES, 2007), this phase is to be covered in Year 1 (Primary 2).

(i) Spelling alternatives and a sample Phase 5 lesson

Phase 5 introduces children to the complexities of the English spelling system. Some vowel sounds can be represented in alternative ways, e.g. the long vowel sound /ā/ can be represented by **ai** (train), **ay** (play), **a – e** (gate), **eigh** (eight), **ey** (obey), and **ei** (reins); these are known as spelling alternatives. The new graphemes for reading for Phase 5, in Weeks 1–4, are shown in Table 7.4 below. It is recommended that you teach about four per week, so a line represents one week's teaching.

Table 7.4 Phase 5: Vowel and consonant digraphs, irregular and high-frequency words

Phase 5	Vowel and consonant digraphs (to be taught also in the context of words)				Irregular/high-frequency words
5.1	ay	oy	wh	a-e	oh, their
5.2	ou	ir	ph	e-e	people, Mr, Mrs
5.3	ie (pie)	ue (Sue)	ew (new)	i-e	looked, called, asked
5.4	ea (eat) zh (treasure)	aw au (Paul)	oe (toe)	o-e u-e (tube)	Revise preceding words

We are now going to show you how to teach the vowel digraph **oy** from Phase 5 (see Table 7.4 above), using the basic Phase 2 lesson plan described in Chapter 6 (where we used the letter **d**).

Introduction	Share the daily targets and criteria for success with the children. Use your structured guide or lesson notes to prompt you for the sequence of the lesson. Display an outline sheet[1] for the children's benefit.
Revision	Revisit the /oi/ sound from Phase 3 (which is the same sound as for **oy**). Ask the children to: read the words (blending if needed) e.g. **oil, joint, soil, coins** segment and spell the words for you to write on the board e.g. **coil, boil, spoil, join** spell previous irregular/high-frequency words e.g. **said, so, come, like**
Teach	'oy' sounds the same as the previous learned sound /oi/; pronounce and find the vowel digraph position in words **toy, employ, annoy** and **Joy**. the syllable blending strategy for reading two-syllable words[2] e.g. **enjoy** the syllable blending strategy for spelling two-syllable words[2] e.g. **ahoy** irregular and high-frequency words, reading and spelling e.g. **oh, their**
Practise	reading **oy** words e.g. **oyster, royal** spelling dictated words e.g. **joy, tomboy** spelling picture words e.g. **boy, toys**
Apply	read the sentence e.g. **We like to go to the play park.** write the sentence e.g. **Joy and Roy can come with me.**
Assessing learning outcomes against success criteria	Plenary Session with the children. From your own observations you will know what the children have achieved. You now want to know what the children think they have achieved. Would they give themselves a happy face or a sad face? If a sad face, perhaps this is where there is a problem to be addressed. Children should be able to: give the correct sound for given graphemes write the grapheme correctly for given sounds use the blending strategy for reading two-syllable words use the blending strategy for spelling two-syllable words read a sentence which includes an irregular/high-frequency word write a sentence which includes an irregular/high-frequency word, forming the letters correctly
Ongoing formative assessment	From assessing the learning indicated above, you can identify which children might be needing extra support during the programme, whether some extra time might need to be taken to consolidate what has been taught before proceeding to the next lesson, and whether your teaching might need to be adapted.

1   In Chapter 6 (Table 6.2) we gave guidance on how to design a chart for the children that outlines the sections of the lesson, so they can see how the lesson is proceeding.
2   See section (iv) of this chapter below for a description of how we would teach children to blend multi-syllabic words for reading, and to segment them for spelling.

Figure 7.1 Example of actual lesson for Phase 5

(ii) Alternative pronunciations for graphemes

For weeks 5–7 of Phase 5, *Letters and Sounds* (DfES, 2007) concentrates on common alternative pronunciations for graphemes, for example, the soft 'c' as in 'ice' and the soft 'g' as in 'ginger'. Examples of the alternative pronunciations for graphemes recommended for teaching by *Letters and Sounds* are given below in Table 7.5.

Table 7.5 Phase 5: Graphemes with alternative pronunciations, irregular and high-frequency words

Phase 5	Graphemes with alternative pronunciations (to be taught also in the context of words)				Irregular/high-frequency words
5.5	'i' (kind)	'ow' (blow)	'y' (by) (very)	'o' (cold)	eyes, any, many, because
5.6	'ie' (field)	'ch' (chef) (school)	'c' (pencil)	'ea' (bread)	again, once, please, friends
5.7	'ou' (could) (shoulder) (you)	'g' (ginger)	'er' (her)	'u' (put) 'a' (what)	work, where, different, laughed water, thought, through, mouse, who

(iii) Alternative spellings for phonemes

For weeks 8–30 of Phase 5, *Letters and Sounds* continues with˘

- **practising and consolidating previous learning;**
- **reading and spelling words with adjacent consonants;**
- **reading and spelling both high-frequency words and multi-syllabic words;**
- **reading and writing sentences.**

In addition, the concept of alternative spellings for phonemes is now introduced. For example, the target phoneme is /m/ but the spelling is 'lamb', the target sound is /z/ but the spelling is 'cheese'. *Letters and Sounds* provides banks of words and sentences which can be used in the same way as we demonstrated in the lesson for teaching the vowel digraph **oy**.

(iv) Syllabification

During Phases 2 to 4, the children will have learnt to work with individual letters, sounding and blending successive letters to read words, and segmenting phonemes to spell words. Even when words of more than one syllable were introduced, e.g. 'wigwam', 'zebra', 'anorak', the children will have sounded and blended individual successive letters for reading. However, in this Phase 5 the children now need to learn how to blend syllables together for reading. They also need to learn how to segment words into syllables, before segmenting them in turn into phonemes for spelling. In this section we will outline how we would handle each of these elements.

A syllable is a word or part of a word that can be spoken independently, e.g. 'alphabet' has three syllables, **al/ pha/ bet**. Recognition of syllables, and breaking words into syllables, is important for both reading and spelling. Pupils need to know that:

- **all words have at least one syllable;**
- **each syllable has one vowel sound (vowel digraphs counting as one vowel);**
- **long words are made up of short syllables;**
- **syllables can be one letter or a group of letters, one of which must be a vowel sound (including 'y' used as a vowel).**

REFLECTIVE TASK

Task 2 Syllabification

Insert each word from the list of words in the following table into the appropriate column and indicate the syllable splits in the words. (Answers at the end of the chapter.)

Words			One syllable	Two syllables	Three syllables
Ruth	Alison	Philip	Ruth	Phil/ip	Al/is/on
circle	hexagon	cube			
elephant	horse	rabbit			
apple	celery	grape			
barbecue	quiche	kebab			

From the above activity, you will have noticed, for example, that 'cube' is only one syllable. This is because the silent 'e', although a vowel, does not count as a syllable. There are recognised rules for where to split words into syllables, which you will find in Appendix 4.

In Phase 5, the children need to learn to tackle multi-syllabic words for reading and spelling by breaking them down into their component syllables. We would teach these skills to children by:

- **showing them how to divide words into syllables visually for reading;**
- **showing them how to divide words auditorily into syllables (and then into phonemes) for spelling;**
- **showing them how to apply the skills in the latter when writing to dictation sentences containing polysyllabic words.**

Reading words of more than one syllable, children will:

See the printed word and will need to be able to:	**bedroom**
• separate the target printed word into syllables	bed / room
• sound and blend successive letters of each syllable	/b/ /e/ /d/ → /bed/
	/r/ /oo/ /m/ → /room/
• sound and blend successive syllables to read the word	/bed/ /room/ → bedroom
• read the whole two-syllable word	**bedroom**

Spelling words of more than one syllable, children will:

Hear the target word and will need to be able to:

- pronounce the target word   /bedroom/
- break the word into syllables, pronounce each syllable   /bed/ /room/
- sound and write the successive letters of each syllable,   /b/ /e/ /d/ → /bed/
  and then blend them to check the letter order   /r/ /oo/ /m/ → /room/
- sound and blend the successive syllables to spell and say   /bed/ /room/ → bedroom
- spell the target word orally using the letter names   'b' 'e' 'd' 'r' 'o' 'o' 'm'
                                          spells **bedroom**

As regards the dictation of sentences, in our programme *Fast Phonics First* (Watson and Johnston, 2007) we suggest a procedure you can follow for the dictation of a sentence.

- **Revise the specific aspect being stressed within the sentence, e.g. the taught graphemes, irregular words, multi-syllabic words, and so on. If the purpose of the sentence is to include a word with more than one syllable, you may feel you need to go over the procedure we described above for breaking up the word into the syllables. (If you use the board to demonstrate this, remember to clear it before starting the activity.)**
- **Slowly and distinctly dictate the sentence to the children.**
- **Ask them to repeat the sentence together.**
- **Dictate the sentence again slowly and distinctly and ask the children to write it. Pause to give the children time to do this. You may need to dictate the sentence again, slowly and distinctly.**
- **Ask some of the children to assist you in writing the sentence on the board by telling you which letters to write for the words.**
- **Ask one child to read the completed sentence.**
- **You and the children can compare their sentences with the one on the board.**

(C) Phase 6: introducing morphemes

In Phase 6, children learn to think about segmenting words into meaningful units, i.e. *morphemes*. Morphemes are the smallest units of meaning in language and consist of one or more phonemes. A root or base word can stand alone, and is a morpheme in its own right (e.g. 'turn'). It can have a prefix (e.g. 'return') or a suffix (e.g. 'turning') or both a prefix and a suffix (e.g. 'returning'). If children learn to recognise larger segments in unfamiliar words, such as morphemes, this will aid the fluency and automaticity of their word reading.

(i) Suffixes

A suffix is a morpheme which can be a letter or a group of letters and is added after a word; below are examples of suffix morphemes attached to root words.

- *-s* **(dog/dogs) provides information – there is more than one dog;**
- *-es* **(box/boxes) provides information – there is more than one box;**
- *-ing* **(waiting) provides information – this is happening in the present;**
- *-ed* **(waited) provides information – this happened in the past.**

BEETFECLIAE 1V2K
REFLECTIVE TASK

Task 3

Try adding your own examples of suffix and prefix morphemes to the following tables.

Table 7.6 below shows some more examples of how suffixes can be added to root words.

Table 7.6 Suffix morphemes

Suffix	What it means	Examples
-s	This makes the word plural and means more than one	star/stars
-es (after s, ss)	This makes the word plural and means more than one	bus/buses class/classes
-es (after ch, sh, tch)	This makes the word plural and means more than one	arch/arches wish/wishes watch/watches
-es (after x, z/zz)	This makes the word plural and means more than one	box/boxes buzz/buzzes
-ed	in the past	splash/splashed
-ing	doing now in the present	splash/splashing

(ii) Prefixes

A prefix morpheme can be a letter or group of letters such as 're' and 'un' put before a word. It is usually joined to the word to change its meaning e.g. 'return' (see Table 7.7 below).

Table 7.7 Prefix morphemes

Prefix	What it means	Examples
re-	*again*	build/rebuild
un-	*not*	known/unknown

(D) Pace of delivery of programme

Letters and Sounds (DfES, 2007) envisages the following timetable for Phases 2–6. Phases 2–4 should be completed in the Reception year (Primary 1), and Phase 5 should be taught during Year 1 (Primary 2). Phase 6 is intended to be taught in Year 2 (Primary 3). This latter phase will lend itself to further consolidation of teaching and learning, with reading becoming more fluent and automatic; here children will learn about word structure and spelling, laying the foundation for Key Stage 2 (Primary 4–7). This is the pace we suggest in our programme *Fast Phonics First* (Watson and Johnston, 2007). However, the pace of phonics teaching can be moderated according to the needs of individual classes, as you may have a class that needs extra time for the consolidation of their learning.

We have shown that one lesson format can be used on a daily basis throughout the programme. From the first example, using the single consonant **d** and one-syllable CVC words (shown in Chapter 6), to the second example, using the vowel digraph **oy** with multi-syllable words (this chapter), you can identify the progression:

- from sounding and blending *letters* to sounding and blending *syllables* and *morphemes*;
- from using magnetic letters to using pencil and paper for dictation and spelling;
- building-up of the learning of irregular and high-frequency words;
- learning alternative spellings for phonemes;
- moving from reading captions to sentences, to connected sentences and text.

The continued use of decodable/graded readers will provide opportunities for children to practise reading and to develop fluency in reading.

(E) Curriculum implications

(i) Link to dictionary skills
In Chapter 9, you will read about how positively the Clackmannanshire teachers viewed the effectiveness of our synthetic phonics programme. The fast pace meant that many other aspects of the curriculum could be introduced earlier. For example, the children had knowledge about the alphabet, both lower and upper case letters and alphabetic order, right from the start of school. From there it was found that this knowledge could serve as a foundation for learning dictionary skills at an earlier stage than would previously have been the case. Activities such as placing words in alphabetical order, and using words beginning with different letters, served as preparation for being able to start looking up words in a dictionary, and learning about the function of a dictionary. We have included such activities in our programme *Fast Phonics First* (Watson and Johnston, 2007).

(ii) Link to school and class forward planning
We find that with our programme, the structure and format are such that it lends itself not only to *detailed weekly planning*, but also to *detailed daily planning*. The ongoing formative assessment element means that children needing extra support can easily be identified and given support within their class. At some stage, a Support for Learning (SfL) teacher may need to be involved. If so, an *individual learning programme* can be devised for joint implementation between the SfL teacher and the class teacher. You will be able to read about such co-operation in the Case Study in Chapter 8.

A SUMMARY OF **KEY POINTS**

> As there are more speech sounds than there are letters of the alphabet (Morris 1990), the concept of consonant and vowel digraphs, e.g. 'chop', 'coat', is discussed.

> We include tables illustrating the *Letters and Sounds* (DfES, 2007) order for teaching consonant and vowel digraphs and irregular and high-frequency words in Phase 3, and adjacent consonants in Phase 4.

> A sample implementation of a lesson demonstrating how to teach a Phase 5 vowel digraph is included (using the same format as the basic lesson plan for teaching a Phase 2 single letter in Chapter 6).

> We include tables illustrating an order for teaching the alternative pronunciations for graphemes, the alternative spellings for phonemes, and the irregular and high-frequency words listed in *Letters and Sounds* for Phase 5.

> We cover the concepts of syllabification needed for Phase 5, where the recognition of syllables and the breaking of words into syllables are critical skills for both reading and spelling. Strategies for reading and spelling words of more than one syllable are set out, as is a procedure for dictating sentences for children to write.

> In Phase 6, children learn to think about segmenting words into meaningful units. The concept of morphemes is introduced; root (or base) words, prefix and suffix morphemes are described.
> We explain that dictionary skills can be introduced at an earlier stage than with previous programmes.
> The impact of a very structured phonics programme on school planning procedures is discussed.

Reflective task answers

Task 2: Syllabification.

Insert each word from the list of words in the following table into the appropriate column and indicate the syllable splits in the words.

Words			One syllable	Two syllables	Three syllables
Ruth	Alison	Philip	Ruth	Phil/ip	Al/is/on
circle	hexagon	cube	cube	cir/cle	hex/a/gon
elephant	horse	rabbit	horse	rab/bit	el/e/phant
apple	celery	grape	grape	ap/ple	cel/e/ry
barbecue	quiche	kebab	quiche	ke/bab	bar/be/cue

REFERENCES REFERENCES **REFERENCES** REFERENCES REFERENCES REFERENCES

DfES (2007) *Letters and Sounds*. London: DfES. **www.standards.dfes.gov.uk/local/clld/las.html**

Dunn-Rankin, P. (1968) The similarity of lower case letters of the English Alphabet. *Journal of Verbal Learning and Verbal Behaviour*, 7: 990–95.

Morris, J. (1990) *The Morris-Montessori Word List*. London: The London Montessori Centre.

Primary National Strategy (2006) *The Primary Framework for Literacy and Mathematics: Guidance for practitioners and teachers on progression and pace in the teaching of phonics (Annex B Outline of Progression)*. **www.standards.dfes.gov.uk/primary/features/primary/pri_fwk_corepapers/**

Watson, J. E. and Johnston, R. S. (2007) *Fast Phonics First (part of Rigby Star Phonics)*. Oxford: Harcourt.

8
How to assess and diagnose reading problems – a case study

Learning objectives

In this chapter you will learn:

- **about tests which are available to assess where a child's reading and spelling skills lie in relation to the national average;**
- **how to assess children's phonic difficulties, and how to support their learning to improve their phonic skills;**
- **how all of these approaches were used to help a child with special educational needs achieve a very good standard of word reading and spelling performance.**

Those recommended for Qualified Teacher Status (QTS) should meet the following Professional Standards:

Q12: Know a range of approaches to assessment, including the importance of formative assessment.

Q13: Know how to use local and national statistical information to evaluate the effectiveness of their teaching, to monitor the progress of those they teach and to raise levels of attainment.

Q19: Know how to make effective personalised provision for those they teach, including those for whom English is an additional language or who have special educational needs, and how to take practical account of diversity and promote equality and inclusion in their teaching.

Q26:

    (a) Make effective use of a range of assessment, monitoring and recording strategies.

    (b) Assess the learning needs of those they teach in order to set challenging learning objectives.

Q27: Provide timely, accurate and constructive feedback on learners' attainment, progress and areas for development.

Q28: Support and guide learners to reflect on their learning, identify the progress they have made and identify their emerging learning needs.

Q29: Evaluate the impact of their teaching on the progress of all learners, and modify their planning and classroom practice where necessary.

Chapter overview

(A) Introduction
(B) Assessment of reading and spelling skills.
(C) Assessment of phonic difficulties.
(D) A case study

(A) Introduction

As we showed in Chapter 1, there are very low levels of underachievement when a synthetic phonics programme is well implemented, but inevitably some children will make slow progress and will need a lot of support. As so many children make a good start with synthetic phonics, the number of children needing extra help will be reduced, meaning that more time may be available to devote to slower learners. We are firmly of the view that children who make slow progress in learning to read and spell will need additional support that is closely related to their learning needs, rather than just general support with class activities. Their learning needs can be assessed by looking closely at their phonic difficulties in reading, and by examining their spelling difficulties. Once you have worked out where a child's problems lie you can carry out re-teaching so that they overcome their problems. In this chapter we will chart the progress of a boy with special educational needs who had a support programme tailored to his areas of difficulty.

(B) Assessment of reading and spelling skills

We find it very useful to start by giving children with problems tests that tell us how they are performing compared to the average for their age (see Chapter 1). Many children who learn slowly have problems in recognising the printed word, so we start by administering a single word reading test. We used the British Ability Scales Word Reading Test (Elliott et al., 1977) in our studies, but this has now been updated and BAS11 (Elliott et al., 1996) is available from NFER Nelson (see the end of this chapter for the address). BAS11 includes many sub-tests, but the ones for word reading and spelling are particularly useful. The Word Reading test will tell you whether a child has any independent reading skill, as tests like this consist of a list of unrelated words. The spelling test (Schonell and Schonell, 1952) consisted of words for dictation. For a whole class assessment of reading comprehension we used the Group Reading Test (Macmillan Unit, 2000). However, for a really in-depth individual assessment of reading comprehension the Neale Analysis of Reading Ability (Neale, 1989) is widely used. This gives children a very thorough assessment not only of reading comprehension, but also of reading rate and accuracy when reading text. These are just suggested tests – there are many other excellent tests available which you may already be using.

(C) Assessment of phonic difficulties

The other major type of assessment we use involves working out a child's phonic weaknesses, which helps us develop a teaching programme tailored to the child's needs.

Letter-sound learning

First and foremost, it is very useful to measure children's knowledge of letter sounds, as these are the building blocks of phonics. For some children this basic level of learning can be very difficult. We advise you not to test the letter sounds in alphabetical order, as children might have memorised the order but not be able to relate the sounds to the symbols! You can also usefully assess children's ability to write letters to dictation. To help children learn the letter sounds, it may be particularly beneficial to teach them mnemonics, such as characters associated with the letters, or distinctive hand and sound actions, as well as plenty of work forming the letters. All of these activities will help consolidate letters and their sounds in the memory. However, some children will remember the mnemonics and not the sounds when you test their letter knowledge, so this work should be time limited (*Letters and Sounds*, DfES, 2007).

Individual testing of phonics skills

Some children are very slow to learn to sound and blend, even when they know quite a few letter sounds. We do not recommend holding a child back from the classroom phonics programme until he or she has learnt the letter sounds, or can sound and blend, as we have found it beneficial for slower learning children to stay in the class programme, where they get plenty of exposure to printed words and to sounding and blending. Joining in with these activities will remind them that when reading unfamiliar words they need to look at letter sounds for useful information, tracking from left to right to decode the words. Staying in the class programme will also aid their vocabulary development. However, they can do additional work with other slow learners at other times during the day, to help them keep up.

Assessing blending skills

We recommend that to assess blending skills the children read nonwords (i.e. made-up words) that test their knowledge of what is taught in each phase. The reason we recommend nonwords is that if you show a child real words they may be words that the child has learnt to recognise by sight without having grasped the phonic skill that you are checking. In our programme *Fast Phonics First* (Watson and Johnston, 2007) we have devised nonwords to use to diagnose phonic difficulties. For example, blending skills can be assessed by asking the children to read simple CVC nonwords, such as 'kug' or 'lan'. It is very useful to take notes on how they tackle this task, to get an idea of what their problems are.

- **If the children give you a real word, they may not have understood the task, in which case you can read a few nonwords for them to show them what is wanted.**
- **If they still cannot read any nonwords, but in other tests you have found that they know the letter sounds, they may have got the idea that they can read an unfamiliar word from its visual appearance without working systematically through the letter sounds.**
- **If the children go sequentially through the letter sounds and are still not be able to come up with a pronunciation of the nonword, then they are having difficulty in blending.**

We recommend with all of these difficulties that the child spends some time 'reading' nonwords to master the principle of sounding and blending, as only a phonic approach will lead to a successful outcome with nonwords, whereas real words may already be known by the child.

Early on, you can test children for their reading of simple CVC nonwords, e.g. 'hig'. It is also useful to test for their ability to blend nonwords containing adjacent consonants, e.g 'sned', 'frod'; these are longer and more demanding. We also recommend, as the class progresses through the phases, assessing the reading of consonant digraphs, e.g. 'phid', vowel digraphs, e.g. 'boam', 'pone', and the ability to read prefixes and suffixes as whole units, e.g. rebult, kibbing. Most children find vowel digraphs hard to master, and some children who have not previously experienced difficulties may start to have problems. Some suggested nonwords are listed in Appendix 5.

Assessing segmentation skills

You can assess the children's ability to segment spoken words in two ways.

- by pronouncing a word, asking them to repeat it, and then asking them to tell you the sounds from first to last;
- by doing the above, and asking them to select the appropriate magnetic letters.

They may only be able to tell you the first sound, they may miss sounds, or they may get the sounds out of sequence. If this is the problem, you can reinforce segmenting by plenty of oral practice. If the problem arises when they have to choose the appropriate letters, make sure they put down a letter as each sound is segmented, rather than trying to do it all at once. When they have done this, ask them to sound and blend the letters they have selected. At this point, they may notice missing letters or find some letters to be in the wrong order. This approach is, of course, what we recommend to be done in class as well, but working one-to-one with slow learners outside the lesson will help them focus on hearing the sounds in the word.

Group testing of phonic skills

The tests described so far are all designed for individual administration. However, we have also devised tests for spelling (with a reading element) for the busy class teacher to use (Watson and Johnston, 2007). These tests can be given to the whole class, as a screening to see which children are making slow progress. These will help you decide which children need to do the individual nonword reading tests. The children read sentences like:

The dog ran into the ____ (road   rode)

The children get these sentences on printed sheets and circle the correct words. They can work through them in their own time as a class assessment, or the tests can be administered individually, with you reading the sentence frame if need be and the child deciding which is the correct spelling of the word to complete the sentence.

We have produced assessment sheets like these for all of the phonic patterns that children cover from Phase 2 to Phase 6. From Phase 5 onwards, we also specify which units to re-teach, as these sessions largely deal with vowel digraphs, which are, as we have said before, hard for all children to learn.

(D) A case study

We used many of the approaches described above to understand the reading problems of a boy with special educational needs. A fuller description of this case study is given in Johnston and Watson (2005). Anthony started school a year later than his classmates, as he was not ready for school, both socially and emotionally and because he had poor receptive and expressive language. He also had hearing difficulties which affected his speech. He was 5.9 years old when he started school, and he was allocated a Supervisory Assistant to support his learning. His class was in our study in Clackmannanshire, which carried out the analytic phonics plus phonological awareness training programme for two terms (see Chapter 1). This meant his class was learning about letter sounds in the initial position of words (as is typical in analytic phonics in the UK) for 10 minutes a day for 16 weeks, and he also had 10 minutes a day analysing and synthesising sounds in spoken words.

Before the programme started, we tested him on the British Picture Vocabulary Test (Dunn et al., 1982), on which he scored 54 (where the average is 100). This is a test of receptive vocabulary. The child sees a page with four pictures on, the tester says the name of one of them, e.g. 'cup', and the child has to choose the picture to go with the spoken word. The other children in this group scored an average of 90.2, therefore it was clear that this boy was very much below average in vocabulary knowledge. We gave also him the BAS Word Reading Test (Elliott et al., 1977), and the Schonell Spelling test (Schonell and Schonell, 1952); he got no scores on these tests, but neither did the other children in this group. He did know a few letter names, but less than the others in his group, and he knew no letter sounds. We found he could not say any of the sounds in spoken words (e.g. what are the sounds in 'zoo'?), and he could not provide any rhymes (e.g. what rhymes with 'hop'?). However, many other children in the study also started out with no reading, spelling, letter knowledge, phoneme segmentation or rhyme ability.

REFLECTIVE TASK

Anthony started school with delayed language development and hearing difficulties, and his vocabulary knowledge was well below the average for his age. What are your expectations for his progress in
a) word reading,
b) spelling; and
c) reading comprehension?

The analytic phonics plus phonological awareness condition that Anthony was part of learnt 16 letter sounds by March of the first year at school. The other children knew most of them when we did our post-tests, and Anthony knew 11 of them. However, he still could not segment phonemes in spoken words, or give rhyming words, although the other children in the group got about a third of the answers right on these two tests. The other children were reading and spelling around the right level for their age, but Anthony was still not scoring on these tests.

At this point, Anthony and his group started on the synthetic phonics programme. However, in November of Anthony's second year at school, an Individual Educational Programme was devised for him. A particular focus of this programme was his delayed language development. He was taught by a speech therapist and a learning support teacher to help improve his articulation, oral communication, listening and attention skills, and also his understanding of spatial concepts and grammatical structures. There was also work on his sound blending, visual memory, visual discrimination and visual closure, and motor co-ordination skills. We tested both Anthony's and the rest of the group's reading and spelling again in May of the second year at school. The children in this group were now reading 11 months ahead of their age, and spelling around 8.5 months ahead (the mean chronological age was 7.8 years). Anthony had made progress too; he got a score of 5.5 years on the word reading test (at the age of 8.8 years), but did not get a spelling score.

In January of his fourth year at school, he gained a word reading score of 6.8 years, and a spelling age of 7.0 years (when he was aged 9.6 years). He scored 100% on the letter sounds, phoneme segmentation, and CVC nonword reading tests (his group as a whole scored 87% on the letter-sound test, 66.7% on the phoneme-segmentation test, and 87% on the nonword test!). By analysing his reading errors, we found that he was able to use a phonic approach to reading, as the excellent nonword reading score suggests, but he still had some problems with blending. For example, he sounded out /sp/ /or/ /t/ but could not blend the sounds to pronounce the word. We could also see he was using a phonic approach to spelling, for example, writing 'yeer' for 'year'.

A test carried out in March of his fifth year at school showed that he read correctly 91.6% of nonwords with initial consonant blends (e.g. 'glat'), 100% of nonwords with final consonant blends (e.g. 'kust'), 100% of nonwords with vowel digraphs (e.g. 'naik'), and 75% of nonwords with silent 'e's (e.g. 'bime'). (See Appendix 5 for the nonwords we used.) His word reading and spelling was now at the 9 year old level (at the age of 10.3 years). He had worked out for himself that blending at the syllable level was a good strategy with poly-syllabic words, but he still had a few problems such as not knowing where to use **c** or **k** in spelling, or whether **c** had a soft or hard sound in reading.

He had a very good teacher supporting his learning, who carried out her own programme with him, which was similar to a revisiting programme we had offered to schools at that time. She noted that Anthony succeeded in tasks where he followed the systematic, defined procedure used in synthetic phonics, that is, sounding and blending for reading, and segmenting spoken words for spelling. In his sixth year at school, she concentrated on helping him read words with two and three syllables. The procedure was to identify sylla-bles, sound and blend the letters within the syllables, and then blend the syllables together. For spelling, he practised learning to break up words into syllables, spelling each syllable, and then blending the syllables together to check he had the right letters. He also learnt spelling rules and was encouraged to examine whether his spelling 'looked right'; if it did not, he was encouraged to try another digraph having the same sound. Together with the assistance of an occupational therapist, his Support for Learning teacher helped Anthony strengthen his hand-writing skills, but he was also taught to touch type to help him work faster and more efficiently.

Anthony also had a lot of help with his reading comprehension, but when he was 10.6 years old, he was understanding what he read only at a 6.9 year old level. There was no evidence of his word reading being slow and effortful, as on a test of how many words he could read in a minute his performance was average (Nicolson and Fawcett, 1998), so this is an unlikely explanation of his poor reading comprehension. We did not assess his listening skills, but given his language problems it is very likely that they were below the average for his age; that is, it is likely that he would have shown poor comprehension of spoken sentences. His Support for Learning teacher devised a series of progressive procedures for comprehension that Anthony could follow to help him read with understanding, based on the fact that he did well when he had clear procedures to follow. She worked on getting him to identify a sentence in a piece of text, to highlight key word(s), read the key word, read around the key word, return to the beginning of the sentence and read it again. She then asked him questions about the meaning of the sentence. However, even at the end of his seventh year at school he was still only showing reading comprehension at the 7.1 year old level. Below we show a table that charts Anthony's progress from the third to the seventh year at school.

Table 8.1 Anthony's reading and spelling at the end of the third, fifth and seventh years at school

	Third year at school	Fifth year at school	Seventh year at school
Chronological age	8.8	10.6	12.6
Word reading age	5.5	9.2	12.4
Spelling age	0.0	8.9	11.2
Reading comprehension	–	6.9	7.1

Did you predict this pattern of performance when you did the reflective task?

Anthony made excellent progress in word reading and spelling. Given that by the seventh year at school his classmates were on average aged 11.6 years, his performance in word reading and spelling was very creditable indeed, as he had worked his way up to the level of performance that was expected for his age. However, his reading comprehension was still well below the average for his age; his score of 7.1 years can be converted into a standard score of 72 (where the average is 100). On a test of vocabulary knowledge taken at the end of his sixth year at school, he only gained a standard score of 63 (up from 54 when he started school). Vocabulary knowledge is more closely associated with reading comprehension than word reading and spelling, so despite Anthony's excellent progress in word reading and spelling, his impaired language skills were an impediment to him developing good reading comprehension.

However, despite his low ability, the synthetic phonics approach, together with considerable learning support, helped him develop word reading and spelling skills appropriate for his age. There is a view that we have often heard expressed that children with special educational needs cannot learn by a phonics approach. We have shown that this need not be the case, and that persisting with the synthetic phonics method and giving appropriate learning support can lead to an excellent outcome.

A SUMMARY OF KEY POINTS

> Standardised tests of word reading, spelling and reading comprehension can be carried out to find out where a slow learner is performing in relation to other children of the same age.

> Diagnostic tests of phonic skill can be carried out to pinpoint slow learners' areas of difficulty.

> These phonic diagnostic tests can be used as the basis of an individually devised learning support programme.

> Even a child with marked language problems was able to read words and spell well using the synthetic phonics approach, and with a considerable amount of learning support tailored to his needs.

REFERENCES REFERENCES **REFERENCES** REFERENCES REFERENCES REFERENCES

DfES (2007) *Letters and Sounds.* London: DfES. www.standards.dfes.gov.uk/local/clld/las.html

Dunn, Ll. M., Dunn, L. M., Whetton, C. and Pintillie, D. (1982) *British Picture Vocabulary Scale.* Windsor: NFER Nelson.

Elliott, C. D., Murray, D. J., and Pearson, L. S. (1977). *The British Abilities Scale.* Windsor: NFER Nelson.

Elliott, C. D, Smith, P. and McCullouch, K (1996) *British Ability Scales II.* Windsor: NFER Nelson.

Johnston, R. S. and Watson, J. (2005) The effects of synthetic phonics teaching on reading and spelling attainment, a seven year longitudinal study. Published by the Scottish Executive Education Department. **www.scotland.gov.uk/Publications/2005/02/20688/52449**

Macmillan Unit (2000) *The Group Reading Test II.* Windsor: NFER Nelson.

Neale, M. D. (1989) *The Neale Analysis of Reading Ability* (Revised). Windsor: NFER Nelson.

Nicolson, R and Fawcett, A (1998) One Minute Reading Test, in *Dyslexia Early Screening Test.* Oxford: Harcourt.

Schonell, F. J. and Schonell, F. E. (1952) *Diagnostic and Attainment Testing* (2nd edition). Edinburgh: Oliver & Boyd.

Watson, J. E. and Johnston, R. S. (2007) *Fast Phonics First* (part of Rigby Star Phonics). Oxford: Harcourt.

Useful address for buying reading and spelling tests

NFER Nelson
The Chiswick Centre
414 Chiswick High Road
London, W4 5TF
Tel: 0845 602 1937
www.nfer-nelson.co.uk/

9
Teachers' views of the synthetic phonics programme

Learning objectives

In this chapter you will see that teachers in Clackmannanshire reported that they:

- **thought that the teaching of reading, spelling and writing had become more accelerated in Primary 1 (Reception) since the synthetic phonics programme started;**
- **thought that since the programme started they had higher expectations of the level that could be achieved in reading, spelling and writing in Primary 1 (Reception);**
- **thought that the children needing support for their learning were detected earlier than they had been before.**

Those recommended for the award of Qualified Teacher Status (QTS) should meet the following Professional Standard.

Q29: Evaluate the impact of their teaching on the progress of all learners, and modify their planning and classroom practice where necessary.

Introduction

You will have seen in Chapter 1 that the children who studied by the synthetic phonics method in Clackmannanshire learnt to read and spell very well, continuing to improve their skills long after the intervention ended.

At the end of the seven-year longitudinal study, a questionnaire was distributed to each of the eight schools in the study to find out the teachers' reactions to using a synthetic phonics programme. The teachers' responses are as follows:

1 *Do you feel that the teaching of reading, spelling and writing has become more accelerated in Primary 1 (Reception) since the synthetic phonics programme started?*

School	Teachers' Responses
1	Yes, definitely accelerated. However, for the last two years, composite classes have had to be used and this type of management slowed down the pace.
2	Yes. Best results ever achieved – never seen before in 30 years of teaching. One child writing own story aged 4. Writing and spelling amazing. I would normally have expected such work at Primary 3 (Year 2) stage. Children also very motivated (Primary 2, i.e. Year 1, teacher).
3	Yes.
4	Yes, without doubt. Teachers, pupils and parents enjoy the challenging pace, the systematic approach and the daily routine.

5	Yes. There is a quicker pace to the teaching of phonics and writing. The reading scheme was introduced six years ago and complements the skills taught in the synthetic phonics programme.
6	Yes. Previously only worked on 26 single sounds in Primary 1 (Reception) – blending didn't start to Primary 2 (Year 1). Holistic approach has seen acceleration and improved attainment in reading/spelling scores.
7	Yes.
8	Children read faster, using phonological awareness to aid independent writing. Care should still be taken to balance pace of lessons, consolidation and retention. Children have more ownership and understanding of why they need sounds and how they read.

2 *Do you feel that since the programme started teachers have higher expectations of the level that can be achieved in reading, spelling and writing in Primary 1 (Reception)?*

School	Teachers' Responses
1	Teachers do have higher expectations though it can depend on the teacher e.g. a late entrant to teaching and a composite class.
2	Yes. Children are reading earlier because they are blending the sounds that they know. Improved confidence is helping their spelling and writing too.
3	Yes.
4	Yes. When staff are challenged, this helps to motivate them to challenge pupils.
5	Yes, there has been a raising of overall expectations of the children. This is especially so with children who require additional support in these areas.
6	Definitely. Building on success and earlier intervention to support less able pupils keep up with the pace and this is paying dividends. We know our children can achieve therefore don't make excuses e.g. 'this is an area of deprivation'. We make a difference and we can prove it!
7	Expectations were raised initially. The accelerated pace of teaching and learning became the norm. Over seven years the pace has varied.
8	Much higher expectations but with the appropriate supports given as suggested in the programme and use of personal judgment.

3 *Do you feel that children needing learning support are detected sooner? At what stage are they identified now and at what stage would they have been typically identified before the programme started?*

School	Teachers' Responses
1	We have always tried to identify children needing learning support as early as possible, usually before Christmas. However with the synthetic phonics programme we can now recognise whether the problems are auditory/visual.
2	Yes. Children are now being identified by the end of the Christmas term in Primary 1 (Reception). Before the programme started this was probably not done until the end of Primary 1 (Reception) and into Primary 2 (Year 1).
3	Yes. We are monitoring progress in Primary 1 (Reception) and beginning catch-up groups in the summer term. Learning Support in place for children by early

Primary 2 (Year 1). Often this would have been Primary 3 (Year 2) before the programme started.

4   Yes. Identified pre-Christmas. Prior to the programme, pre-Easter.

5   Due to the steps in teaching phonics, we are able to offer support earlier by utilising our support staff in activities modelled in class by teachers. We have found that for some children this 'catch-up' group situation whereby they have an additional 10 minutes support time regularly is all that is required to support their learning.

6   Yes. Support for Learning is involved in providing support for those pupils who require extra reinforcement or who have had a period of absence (necessary because of pace of programme) in flexible groups from November of Primary 1 (Reception) onwards. Previously Support for Learning intervention would have been at the beginning of Primary 2 (Year 1) because pace of teaching was so slow in Primary 1 (Reception).

7   Gains are identified clearly due to having baseline assessments. Any children who are not gaining in line with expectations are noticed quickly. Teachers would use a range of informal/formal assessments, professional judgment being to the fore. Children would be identified as they are currently – what we would have done about it is another question.

8   Yes. By the end of the first set of letters children who may have difficulty can be highlighted. By Christmas some of these children will no longer be a concern as they needed time to settle and adapt to school. By January, Primary 1 (Reception), it is very clear who will need significant support.

4 *Please add any other comments you would like to make.*

School	Teachers' Responses
1,2,3	No extra comments.
4	Synthetic phonics sets the standard.
5	We have found the synthetic approach very positive and effective. Our pupils in Primaries 1 to 3 (Reception to Year 2) continue to achieve steadily. We continue to review and monitor the learning and teaching programme in this area and the support strategies that we have in place.
6	Involvement with synthetic phonics was a professional 'life-changing' experience that changed the teaching of English language in our school.
7	The children are very good decoders and encoders to a certain level. Comprehension levels are not in line with the decoding and encoding skills.*
8	Synthetic phonics has provided staff development opportunities alongside curricular development and has empowered both teachers and pupils.

* Authors' note: It should be noted that there are factors that limit the development of reading comprehension, but which have less effect on word reading and spelling skills. These factors include listening comprehension, verbal ability, general knowledge and memory (see Chapter 3 for the association between listening and reading comprehension). However, despite the Clackmannanshire sample being of below average verbal ability, reading comprehension was found to be significantly ahead of chronological age at the end of the study (see Chapter 1).

A SUMMARY OF **KEY POINTS**

> It can be seen that the teachers in the Clackmannanshire study found that:
> – the children's literacy skills were much improved;
> – the less able pupils seemed to gain particular benefit;
> – the children experiencing difficulties could be detected much earlier than they were before.
> It is also evident that the teachers now had a much higher expectation of what their pupils could achieve.

REFERENCES REFERENCES **REFERENCES** REFERENCES **REFERENCES** REFERENCES

Much of the material in this chapter previously appeared in:

Johnston, R. S. and Watson, J. (2005) *The effects of synthetic phonics teaching on reading and spelling attainment, a seven year longitudinal study.* Published by the Scottish Executive Education Department. **www.scotland.gov.uk/Publications/2005/02/20688/52449**

Glossary

Adjacent consonants: another term for this is consonant blends; it refers to a sequence of consonants at the beginning or end of words, e.g. clap, string, post.

Alphabetic code: this refers to the fact that in English spelling the sounds of the spoken words are represented by letters.

Analytic phonics: this starts by teaching letter sounds at a slow rate (e.g. one a week), in the initial position of words. For example, to teach the letter 'c', children would be shown a series of alliterative words, e.g. 'cat', 'car'. They would then be introduced to the letters at the ends of word, e.g. 'nap', 'cup', and then in the middle, e.g. 'cat', 'big'. At this stage, they might be taught to sound and blend. Subsequently initial constant blends, e.g. 'bl', 'cr', final consonant blends, e.g. 'rt', 'lp', and then vowel and consonant digraphs, e.g. 'ee', 'ch', would be taught.

Consolidated alphabetic reading: a child recognises larger elements such as morphemes, seeing for example that 'danced' is composed of two morphemes 'dance' and 'ed'.

Consonant: all the letters of the alphabet except the vowels a, e, i, o, u.

Consonant blends: another term for this is adjacent consonants; it refers to a sequence of consonants at the beginning or end of words, e.g. clap, string, post.

Consonant digraphs: this is where two consonants are needed to spell one sound, 'shop', 'chip', 'them'.

Decodable books: these consist of words using the letter sounds that the children have been taught so far. This means that the children can decode (or sound and blend) words in the book with which they are not familiar. There may also be some tricky words, which the teacher will explain how to pronounce before the children start each book. New books are introduced as more graphemes are taught. Decodable books for Phase 3 will have a less restricted set of words than decodable books for Phase 2, as more graphemes will have been learnt.

Decoding: you can decode (sound and blend) many English words by using the sounds of the letters to work out the pronunciation. Many words are *fully decodable*, e.g. 'hat', and some are *partially decodable* (i.e. the spelling is irregular), e.g. 'said'.

Full alphabetic phase of reading: a child makes connections between letters and sounds all through the word, e.g. the child reads the unfamiliar word 'pat' correctly.

Grapheme: a grapheme is the written representation of a phoneme. Single letters are graphemes, e.g. 't', 'h', but these letters together are also a grapheme, 'th'. For example, the word 'thick' has five letters but only three phonemes 'th' 'i' 'ck'. The term grapheme-phoneme correspondences (GPC) includes letter-sound correspondences, but the latter term refers to the situation where only one letter is needed to represent the sound.

High-frequency words: words which occur frequently in written English (i.e. are commonly used). Some of these have regular and some have irregular spellings.

Irregular words: these words have spellings that give a less than perfect guide to pronunciation. There are two types:

a) Exception words have common spelling patterns (e.g. 'pint', 'have') but their pronunciations differ to most of the words that have similar spellings. For example, 'pint' does not rhyme with 'tint', 'hint', 'splint'; 'have' does not rhyme with 'gave', 'slave', 'wave'. In *Letters and Sounds* (DfES, 2007) these are referred to as 'tricky' words.

b) Strange words words have unique spellings (e.g. 'yacht', 'gauge', 'aisle') and so are not fully decodable, but have some letter sound-information that corresponds with their pronunciation. In *Letters and Sounds* these are referred to as 'tricky' words.

Letter-sound correspondences: the association between the visual representations of letters and their sounds (not their names). Also covered by the term grapheme-to-phoneme correspondences.

Logographic writing system: a writing system like Chinese, in which individual characters stand for words, but do not represent them pictorially.

Multi-sensory: using sight, touch, and sound for learning, particularly of letters.

Morphemes: are the smallest units of meaning in language and consist of one or more phonemes. All morphemes have meaning, but that meaning can be grammatical. For example, the word 'dog' is a morpheme. We can add the grammatical morpheme 's' to indicate more than one dog, i.e. 'dogs'. A suffix is a morpheme which is added after a word, e.g. 'ing' in 'playing', which means that play is happening now in the present. In the word 'played', the 'ed' means that play happened in the past. A prefix is a morpheme where letters are put before a word to change its meaning, e.g. 'dis' in 'dislike' means not, that is, you do not like something.

Nonwords: these are invented words which follow the rules of English spelling. Examples are 'hib', 'flont', 'brin'.

Partial alphabetic phase of reading: a child uses some letter-sound information when reading, often the beginning and/or end letters of words, e.g. a child identifies 'tin' as 'toy'.

Phoneme: this is the smallest sound unit in a word which makes a difference to the word's meaning. For example, you can change the meaning of 'rat' by changing the first phoneme – 'cat', 'mat', 'hat', 'sat'. Therefore /c/, /m/, /h/, /s/ are all phonemes. The term 'phoneme' only refers to sounds, not to written representations (which are graphemes).

Phonics: a method of teaching reading that capitalises on the fact that English spelling is alphabetic. Letter-sound information is used to help pronounce unfamiliar words.

Pre-alphabetic phase of reading: a child reads words by salient visual cues and does not look at the letters. It is sometimes referred to as logographic reading. For example, a child may recognise 'Pepsi' correctly when the word is presented with its logo and distinctive lettering. However, if the letter 'p' is replaced by the letter 'x', so it is shown as 'Xepsi', the child still reads it as 'Pepsi'.

Phonemic awareness: the ability to perceive and manipulate the phonemes in *spoken* words. If you were testing a child's explicit phoneme awareness, you would read out words to them, and they would tell you the phonemes in the word. That is, they would tell you that the spoken word 'cat' has the sounds /c/ /a/ /t/. They would not be looking at the printed words while they were doing this task.

Phonological awareness: the ability to perceive and manipulate the sounds of spoken words. It includes the smallest level, phonemes, but also larger units, such as rimes and syllables.

Onset: the onset is the first part of the word, the consonant(s) before the vowel, e.g. in 'bring' the onset is 'br'.

Regular words: the pronunciations of these words are predictable on the basis of simple grapheme to phoneme conversion rules, for example, 'cat', 'best', 'hand'. These words are completely decodable through sounding and blending.

Rime: the rime of a word is the vowel and the rest of the syllable, e.g. in 'bring' the rime is 'ing'.

Segmentation for spelling: the ability to split a spoken word into phonemes, and to select the letter(s) for each phoneme in order to spell the word.

Sight-word reading: there are many uses of this term. It can refer to a global recognition of words where little use is made of letter-sound information (sometimes called logographic reading). However, Ehri describes how sight-word reading becomes more mature during reading development by being increasingly underpinned by letter-sound information. She also proposes that even when a word becomes very familiar, and can be recognised without overtly using the letter sounds, we still activate not only its whole word pronunciation, but all the possible connections between letters and sounds.

Simple view of reading: reading comprehension can be predicted by multiplying together the ability to (a) recognise and decode printed words, and (b) to understand spoken language.

Sounding and blending for reading: when trying to read an unfamiliar word the child generates the sounds of the letters (or graphemes) from left to right, and then blends them together to find out how the word is pronounced.

Syllables: a syllable is a word or part of a word that can be spoken independently. For example, 'alphabet' has three syllables, al/pha/bet. Syllables can be spelt by one letter or a group of letters (e.g. 'a', 'cat', 'boat','my'). All words have at least one syllable and each syllable has one vowel sound (vowel digraphs count as one vowel, and 'y' can count as a vowel).

Synthetic phonics: starts by teaching children a small group of letter sounds very rapidly, e.g. s, a, t, i, p, n. Children sound and blend words made of up of the taught letters to find out how to pronounce them. Then another letter sound is taught, and children sound and blend new words made up of the previously taught letters. This process continues until all of the letter sounds, digraphs etc, used in English, have been taught.

Tricky words: these are irregular words, where the letter sounds do not provide a perfect guide to pronunciation, e.g. 'said'.

Vowels: There can be as many as 20 vowels in spoken English (the number depends on accent). These are represented in spelling by the letters of the alphabet a, e, i, o, u, either singly or in pairs (see vowel digraphs below). Sometimes 'y' can be used as a vowel, e.g. in 'my'.

Vowel digraphs: some vowel sounds are spelt using two vowels, e.g. 'oa' in 'coat'. A special set of vowel digraphs are variously called silent 'e', magic 'e', or split digraphs. These terms all refer to where the sound of a vowel is lengthened by adding an 'e' after the final consonant, e.g. 'late', 'cube'.

Whole language: The whole language approach grew from work by Ken Goodman in the 1960s; his work led to the idea that children did not need to learn to decode unfamiliar words using the letter sounds, but that they could be guessed from context. Frank Smith thought that children should be immersed in 'real books', the view being that 'children learn to read by reading'.

Appendix 1: Phoneme Awareness Training Programme

Throughout this training programme children are never shown the letters that represent the sounds that are being learnt. We recommend the use of a hand puppet to demonstrate the procedures. For Lessons 1, 2, 3, 7 and 8 the children will need sheets with 2-box phoneme frames. They will also need pencils or crayons to mark their sheets with large dots to signify phonemes.

Lesson 1: Segmenting the initial phoneme in spoken words

Note: " " denotes the whole spoken word, / / denotes the sounds.

1. Explain to the children that they are going to play with the first sound in words; the puppet and children will need to listen very carefully for the first sound of each word.

2. Present a three-box phoneme frame, as below, which can be drawn in chalk on the blackboard. Make a puppet slide a finger under the three squares of the frame saying "mop" in an elongated way. Ask the puppet for the first sound, the puppet says "The first sound in "mop" is /m/ " and points to the first box. Ask the puppet to put in a large dot.

3. Repeat the process for the word "hop" asking one of the pupils to assist the puppet.

4. Repeat the process for the word "cat" asking one of the children to perform without the help of the puppet (unless required).

5. Repeat the process with all of the children marking their sheets with a large dot for the first sound of the words in the list as you go through each word. Give support in saying the first sound if necessary.

Word list

The letters between slash marks indicate it is the sound as it occurs at the start of the word that is to be used, not the letter name.

top – /t/	dad – /d/
pot – /p/	cut – /c/
nip – /n/	get – /g/
it – /i/	leg – /l/
sat – /s/	fun – /f/
rip – /r/	old – /o/
mug – /m/	bit – /b/

At the end of the lesson remind the children of what has been learnt, i.e. to say the first sound heard at the beginning of a word.

Lesson 2: Segmenting the final phoneme in spoken words

First of all revise initial sound segmentation from the previous lesson.

Now the children will learn to say the last sound of a word, represented by the last square of the frame.

1. Explain that they are going to play with the last sound in words; the puppet and children will need to listen very carefully for the last sound of each word.

2. The puppet slides a finger under the three boxes of the frame saying "mop". Ask the puppet what is the last sound, the puppet says /p/. Ask the puppet to point to the last box, say the last sound again, and put in a large dot.

3. Repeat the process for the word "pot", asking one of the pupils to assist the puppet.

4. Repeat the process for "cat" asking one of the pupils to perform without the help of the puppet (unless required).

5. Repeat the process for each of the remainder of the words, asking other children to perform without the help of the puppet (unless required). They should put a dot in the last box as they segment the sound.

top – /p/	dad – /d/	gas – /s/	fill – /l/
bit – /t/	luck – /k	/fur – /r/ (optional)	cough – /f/
fin – /n/	fig – /g/	ham – /m/	cub – /b/

6. Remind the children of what has been learnt, i.e. to hear the sound at the end of words.

Lesson 3 Segmenting first and final phoneme in spoken words

Remind the children that in the previous lesson they found the last sounds in words.

1. Use the three-box frame as before. The puppet slides a finger under the three squares of the frame saying "mop". Ask the puppet what is the first sound of "mop", the puppet says /m/, points to the first box and puts in a large dot.

2. Ask the puppet what is the last sound of the word "mop" and the puppet will say the last sound is /p/, point to the last box and put in a large dot.

3. Repeat the process for the word "pot", asking one of the children to assist the puppet, saying /p/ is the first sound and /t/ is the last sound.

4. Repeat the process for the word "cat" asking one of the pupils to perform without the help of the puppet (unless required), "/c/ is the first sound and /t/ is the last sound."

5. Repeat the process for the following words, asking the children to say the sounds without the help of the puppet (unless required), marking the boxes with large dots.

   Further words and nonwords to work through:

   mac, name, cot, log, book, bim, bat, cos, gob, sip, pub, top, nog, foot, pon, mot, bag, mag, pass, nap, map, tab, pac, sab, cas, toc, gop

   You can explain to the children that nonwords are made up words and do not make sense.

6. Remind the pupils of what has been learnt, i.e. to say the first and the last sound in words.

Lesson 4: Deleting initial and final phonemes and saying what sound is left

The children will learn to segment the final sound and say what is left of the word, and then segment the initial sound and say what is left of the word.

(a) Phoneme segmentation

Say "Now we are going to find the first and last sounds in the word "cot". (Run the puppet's finger under the boxes as you say "cot".)
What is the last sound of "cot"? It's /t/. Put a dot in the last box.
What is the first sound of "cot" ? It's /c/. Put a dot in the first box.

(b) Phoneme deletion

Then say "What sound is left if you take the "c" from "cot"? It's /ot/." Run your finger under the last two boxes as you say /ot/.
"What sound is there if you take the /t/ from "cot"? It's /co/." Run your finger under the first two boxes as you say /co/.

Repeat (a) and (b) using the following examples; begin by finding the first and last sounds (phoneme segmentation), and then say what is left in each word after these sounds are taken off in turn (phoneme deletion).

The segments to pronounce for b) are given below:

> cat –"cat" without the /t/ is /ca/, "cat" without the /c/ is /at/
>
> dip – "dip" without the /p/ is /di/, "dip" without the /d/ is /ip/
>
> sun – "sun" without the /n/ is /su/, "sun" without the /s/ is /un/
>
> fuss – "fuss" without the /s/ is /fu/, "fuss" without the /f/ is /uss/
>
> purr – (optional) "purr" without the /r/ is /pu/, "purr" without the /p/ is /ur/
>
> gum –"gum" without the /m/ is "gu", "gum" without the /g/ is /um/
>
> rod – "rod" without the /d/ is /ro/, "rod" without the /r/ is /od/
>
> tick – "tick" without the /k/ is /ti/, "tick" without the /t/ is /ik/
>
> leg – "leg" without the /g/ is /le/, "leg" without the /l/ is /eg/
>
> fell – "fell" without the /l/ is /fe/, "fell" without the /f/ is /el/
>
> buff – "buff" without the /f/ is /bu/, "buff" without the /b/ is /uff/
>
> sob – "sob" without the /b/ is /so/, "sob" without the /s/ is /ob/
>
> mat – "mat" without the /t/ is /ma/, "mat" without the /m/ is /at/
>
> nap – "nap" without the /p/ is /na/, "nap" without the /n/ is /ap/

Remind the children of what they have learnt today, to take sounds off words and to say what is left.

Lesson 5: Segmenting vowels at the beginning of words

This lesson uses vowel-consonant nonwords (VC). Nonwords are made-up words; you can tell the children that they are made up and do not make sense.

Remind the children that in Lesson 4 they learnt to take the first sound off a word and say what was left, and then to take off the final sound and say what was left.

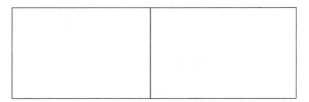

1. Ask the children to listen carefully. You say the word "at", the puppet slides a finger under the two boxes of the frame saying "at". Ask the children to listen for the first sound in "at". The puppet points to the first box and says "The first sound is /a/, /a/ is a vowel." The puppet puts a large dot in the first box.

2. Repeat the process saying the nonword "ag" with a child helping the puppet.

3. Repeat the process with the puppet saying the word "of" and a child pointing to the first box, saying the first vowel sound /o/ independently (helping if necessary).

4. Repeat this process for the series of words listed. In every case the /a/ vowel sound is as in "apple", the /o/ vowel sound is as in "odd", the /i/ sound as in "it", the /u/ sound as in "cup", the /e/ sound as in "get". The children will mark the position of the vowel with a large dot on their phoneme frames.

   List of vowel consonants nonwords to use:

   ot, am, im, eb, ug, ob, ip, ek, ub, em, ak, op, at, ib, ut, es, ik, og, ev, ul, ep, ab, om, ok, as, id, um, ig, un

5. Remind the children of what they have been learning, finding the first vowel sound in short words.

Lesson 6: Segmenting vowels from the end of words

Remind the children that in the previous lesson they learnt to identify vowels at the beginning of nonwords.

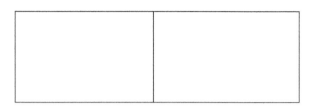

1. Tell the children they are now going to listen for vowels at the end of words. Ask the children to listen carefully. The puppet slides a finger under the frame and says "sa" (pronounced as in "sat"). Ask the children to listen for the last sound in "sa". The puppet points to the last box and says "The last sound is /a/", and puts in a large dot.

2. Repeat the process saying the nonword "po" (as in "pod"), with a child helping the puppet.

3. Repeat the process with the puppet saying the nonword "ma" (as in "mat"), and a child pointing to the last box, saying independently "The last sound is /a/" (help here if necessary).

4. Repeat this process for the series of words listed, with the children putting a large dot in the last box on their sheets as each vowel is segmented. The vowel sounds are pronounced as in Lesson 5.

   CV nonwords:

   pa, ke, nu, ga, bo, te, pu, mi, de, ko, ta, tu, di, le, ba, du, so, si, ga, ne, ru, pa, pi, bu, fe, bo, ki, mo

5. Remind the children of what they have been learning, i.e. segmenting the vowel sound in nonwords.

Lesson 7: Segmenting phonemes in the middle of words

1. Remind the children that they have been listening for vowel sounds as first and last sounds. Tell them today, they are listening for the vowel sounds in the middle of words.

2. Using the three-box frame, say the word "bat", the puppet sliding a finger along underneath while saying the word "bat". Ask the children to listen carefully for the middle sound. Say the word "bat", and ask "What is the middle sound?" The puppet points to the middle box in the frame and says "The middle sound is /a/", and puts a large dot in the middle box.

   If this is difficult, tell the children to take off the first sound and see what is left. "Let's see what "bat" without the /b/ is - it's "at". Now what is "at" without the /t/ – it's /a/."

3. Repeat the process saying the word "fob" with a child helping the puppet. "What is the middle sound in "fob"? It's /o/."

4. Repeat the process with the puppet saying the word "bam". Ask what is the middle sound in "bam". A child independently points to the middle box saying the middle sound is /a /. (Give help where necessary.)

5. Repeat the process for the series of words listed, the children putting a large dot in the middle box of their three-box frames as each vowel is identified.

   Word list

   back, knob, cab, sob, cat, gop, tack, mag, cot, mab, cop, tob, bag, pob, lock,mass, tack, pal, poc, top, pan, hab, mot, tag, cut, mof, pass, sock, tap, pot, net, sun, ant, dog, hat, cup, man, rat

6. Remind the children of what they have been learning, i.e. listening to words and saying the middle sound in each word.

Lesson 8: Segmenting all the phonemes in CVC (consonant-vowel-consonant) words

In this lesson the children will learn to segment the initial, middle and final sounds of words.

Remind the children that last time they were finding the middle sounds of words.

1. Using the three-box frame, say the word "pot", sliding the puppet's finger under the frame. Point to each of the boxes in turn, saying the sounds /p/ /o/ /t/.

2. Repeat the process and when you point to each of the boxes in turn, the puppet says the first sound is /p/, the middle sound is /o/, and the last sound is /t/. Put a large dot in each box as the phoneme is pronounced.

3. Repeat the process for the nonword "tas". The puppet and a child say the first sound is /t/, the middle sound is /a/, and the last sound is /s/.

4. Repeat the process for the word "cab". A child says "The first sound is /c/, the middle sound is /a/ and the last sound is /b/." (Give help where necessary.)

5. Repeat the process with the children filling in the dots on their three-box frames for the words on the list.

    top, cot, bab, mac, sam, bat, got, cat, mac, tom, bot, pot, tam, sap, mat, pat, mag, sog, pom, gop, sot, cag, pos, cog, pob, pub, cab, dig, hen, fat, ant, pan, dog, hat, lum, cos, sog, sop.

6. Remind the children that they have been listening to words and saying what is the first sound, the middle sound and the last sound.

Lesson 9: Auditory blending – blending the last phoneme of a word with the rest of the word, as in 'ca-t'

Remind the children that last time they were learning about finding the first, middle and end sounds in words, using the word "cat" as an example. Now the children are going to blend all the sounds together to make a word.

1. Tell the children they will hear words broken into small parts; they are going to blend these parts together to make a whole word. Ask the children to listen while the puppet slides its finger under the first two boxes, saying /ba/, then under Box 3, saying /g/.

2. Then slide the puppet's finger under all three boxes, saying "bag" in an elongated way but without any breaks. Then say the whole word normally, "bag", and then put it in a sentence, e.g. "Put the towel in the <u>bag</u>."

3. Repeat the process for /ta/ /s/ with the puppet saying the sounds /ta/ /s/ separately, then the whole nonword "tas", then saying "<u>Tas</u> is a nonsense word."

4. Repeat the process with the puppet and a child for the segments /mo/ /p/, saying the sounds separately, then the word "mop" in an elongated way, and then normally "mop", and then a sentence – "We use a <u>mop</u> to clean the floor."

5. Repeat the process for the words in the list:

    ma-ss, go-p, ba-ck, sa-ck, ca-p, ta-g, so-b, to-m. ba-g, ca-t, po-c, ba-m, ga-b, po-t, so-p, ma-p, sa-p, ca-b, ca-t, pa-ck, ga-s, so-b, mo-p, ta-ck, ba-g, pa-ss, so-ck.

6. Remind the children that they have been blending the last sound of the word with the rest of the word.

Lesson 10: Blending initial phonemes with the rest of the word

Remind the children that last time they blended the last sound of a word with the rest of the word.

Say "Today, we are going to blend the first sound of a word with the rest of the word."

1. Ask the children to listen while the puppet slides its finger under one box, saying /c/, and then under the last two boxes, saying /ap/.

2. Slide the puppet's finger under all three boxes saying "cap", followed by a sentence, e.g. "I took off my cap."

3. Repeat the process with the puppet saying the sounds /g/ /om/ and then the nonword "gom", followed by a sentence "Gom is a nonsense word."

4. Repeat the process with the puppet and a child saying the sounds /g/ /as/ and then "gas", finally using the word "gas" in a sentence "We cook using gas."

5. Repeat the process for the words in the list with children saying the sounds and the word, and you giving a sentence. Do not say the whole word first!

    m-at, g-ot, s-ack, c-ap, t-ag, s-ob, t-op, b-ag, c-at, p-oc, b-am, g-ab, p-ass, p-ot, t-ack, s-ock, s-op, m-ap

6. Remind the children that we have been blending the first sound of the word with the rest of the word to make the word.

Lesson 11: Blending three separate phonemes into a word, as in 'c-a-t'

Remind the children that they have been blending the last sound of a word with the rest of the word and the first sound of a word with the rest of the word. Today, they are going to say all three sounds and blend them into a word.

1. Say that the puppet is going to speak in sound-talk, and we are going to work out what it is saying. The puppet says the sounds /m/ /a/ /t/, while pointing to each box in turn. Then the puppet blends the sounds to say "mat."

2. The puppet gives the sounds /h/ /a/ /t/, the children copy the sounds, and then the puppet and the children blend the sounds together.

3. Follow this procedure for each of the words below.

   sun, tap, pin, net, pig, bus, leg, bed, jam, van, mat, ant, hen, fan, cup, fox, tin, cat, dog

4. Remind the children that we have been blending sounds together to find out what the word is.

Lesson 12: Segmenting spoken words into phonemes and blending them back together

Remind the children that last time they sound-talked the words and then blended the sounds together.

Tell the children "You are now going to take a word, cut it up into sound-talk, and then put it back together again. Blending the sounds will change them a bit, but you should still be able to hear them."

1. The puppet says the word "bag".

2. Ask the puppet to put it in sound-talk – the puppet says → /b/ /a/ /g/.

3. Ask the puppet to put it back together. The puppet says "bag" in an elongated way, running its finger under the boxes, and then says "bag" normally.

4. Then the puppet and the children do the same procedure with "gas" → /g/ /a/ /s/. Blend it together in an elongated way, "gas", while the puppet runs its finger under the boxes. Then say "gas" normally.

5. Ask the children what are the sounds in "tap" – see if they can say /t/ /a/ /p/, but help them if they cannot do this. Then ask them to blend the sounds together (assist them if they cannot do this).

   Repeat the procedure with the following words:

   tap, pin, get, rat, man, rim, pat, men, pan, cap, kit, nap, tan, dig, gap, peg, pal, tin, sat, sip, kin, rap, pit, man, rip, mat, leg, tip, can, sit, ran, ten, pen, cat

6. Remind them of what they have been doing in the lesson, blending sounds together to see what the word is.

On the next two pages are some two- and three-box phoneme frames that you can photo-copy to give to the children to use during the lessons.

Name _____ Date_____

Name _____ Date_____

Appendix 2: Score sheet to assess children's knowledge of the letters s a t p

Date:

Child's name	Alphabet knowledge				Can give the sound for:				Can write letters for:			
	song		with print		's'	'a'	't'	'p'	/s/	/a/	/t/	/p/
	Yes	No	Yes	No								

Appendix 3: Score sheet to assess children's ability to sound and blend the letters s a t p

s a t p

Child's name	Blending				Blending				Alphabet				Segmentation		
									Song		Print		Dictation		Picture
	as	at	sap	sat	tap	taps	pat	pats	Y	N	Y	N	pats	taps	tap

Appendix 4: Rules for where to split words into syllables

No.	Rule	Example
1	If two consonants are together between two vowels, the first syllable usually ends **after** the first consonant.*	car ^ ton
		yel ^ low
	(*For dividing a word into syllables, a consonant blend or a consonant digraph is considered as one consonant. Never split up consonant digraphs as they represent only one sound.)	pit ^ cher
		'ch' 'ph' 'sh' 'th' 'th' and 'wh'
2	If a single consonant is between two vowels, it is usually divided **after** the consonant, if the vowel is short.	cab ^ in
		pan ^ ic
3	If a single consonant is between two vowels, it is usually divided **before** the consonant if the vowel is long.	na ^ ture
		be ^ low
4	If a consonant is followed by the ending 'le' the split is **before** the consonant (exceptions: 'ckle' words like pick ^ le).	pur ^ ple
		tum ^ ble
5	When a word has 'ck' or 'x' in it, the split is usually after the 'ck' or 'x'.	pack ^ et
		tax ^ i
6	Initially a compound word is split between the two words making the compound word. If one of those words has more than one syllable another rule is applied.	flash ^ light
		down ^ stairs
7	If two adjoining vowels are sounded separately in a word the syllable split is between the two vowels.	di ^ et
		cru ^ el
8	Vowel digraphs and vowel combinations count as one sound.	count
		dough ^ nut
9	If a syllable ends in a vowel (any vowel) and is the only vowel, it is usually long.	o ^ pen
		pa ^ per
10	If a root word has a prefix, split the word **after** the prefix.	re ^ play
		un ^ load
11	If a root word has a suffix, split the word **between** the root word and the suffix.* (*Except with words like 'shopping' the prefix is 'ping', because when the suffix 'ing' is added to a one-syllable word, the last consonant is doubled before adding 'ing'.)	play ^ ing
		read ^ ing
		shop ^ ping
		swim ^ ming
12	'ed' coming at the end of a word only forms a syllable when preceded by 'd' or 't'.	dart ^ ed
		print ^ ed
13	A syllable ending in a silent 'e' has one and only one consonant before that silent 'e'. Silent 'e' does not count as a syllable.	plan and plane are both one syllable

Appendix 5

Nonwords for testing sounding and blending in Phases 2 and 3

Name:

Date:

Child's response

Child's response

hig		gantok	
nal		muntal	
kug		renbok	
bis		sanlud	
gok		minlan	
dep		ritney	
foy		yomter	
kun		nurdal	
ged		daspog	
lar		ludpon	
jek		bosdin	
lan		culgin	
mip		fambey	
pos		kesdal	
ruk		libnol	
dal		bantik	
ped		lemfid	
fik		mitson	
lom		goklup	
sul		puklon	

Nonwords for assessing phonics skills for Phases 4 and 5

Initial adjacent consonants	**Final adjacent consonants**

Name:

Date:

	Child's response		Child's response
sned	_____	fost	_____
clom	_____	hald	_____
spad	_____	nard	_____
frod	_____	norp	_____
stod	_____	kust	_____
pran	_____	folt	_____
grik	_____	wolp	_____
plud	_____	kants	_____
drot	_____	tirk	_____
smid	_____	jort	_____
glat	_____	lind	_____
flup	_____	benk	_____

Vowel digraph		**Silent 'e'**	
Name:		Date:	
	Child's response		Child's response
pood	_____	dife	_____
kear	_____	noke	_____
yead	_____	cose	_____
dool	_____	wone	_____
yoot	_____	pake	_____
kour	_____	fube	_____
nowd	_____	sode	_____
naik	_____	pone	_____
boam	_____	lude	_____
cait	_____	nade	_____
deak	_____	bime	_____
voim	_____	neke	_____

Some vowel digraphs have multiple acceptable pronunciations, for example, 'kear' could rhyme with 'year' or 'bear'.

Index

Lightning Source UK Ltd.
Milton Keynes UK
UKOW06f0747180813

215518UK00009B/762/P